# ATLANTIS—
## The Mystery Unravelled

# ATLANTIS—
## The Mystery Unravelled

*by*

Jürgen Spanuth

The Book Tree
San Diego, California

Originally published
1956 by ARCO PUBLISHERS LTD
London


New material & revisions
© 2025
The Book Tree
All rights reserved

ISBN 978-1-58509-465-3

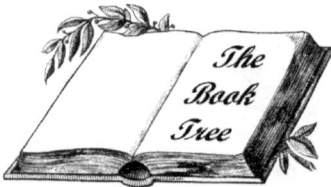

# CONTENTS

## SECTION THREE

## APPENDIX

# LIST OF ILLUSTRATIONS

PAGE

# PREFACE

IN probably no other field of ancient history or geography is research seemingly so barren, but in reality so rewarding, as in that which deals with the problem of Atlantis. The twenty thousand and more volumes, and countless articles, that have already been written on the subject seem to have covered it completely and exhaustively. Eminent scholars have repeatedly claimed to have found the conclusive answer to the riddle and have said that nothing more could usefully be added to the vast literature on the subject; contributors to it have often been treated as cranks and their work dismissed as merely another fact to be chronicled in the history of human folly.

It is of course true that Atlantis has attracted the attention of writers of fiction and others with no claim to a scientific approach, and serious investigators have been exposed to the danger of becoming identified with them. It is not surprising, therefore, that reputable scholars have hesitated to tackle the problem and have left the field largely open to cranks and Atlantomaniacs.

This is the more regrettable since Atlantis offers one of the most fruitful fields of study in ancient history; it lifts the veil of obscurity from one of the most puzzling and eventful epochs in the history of the western world. The legend of Atlantis may be compared to that of the hidden treasure chamber in the tomb of Tutankhamen in the Valley of the Kings. For hundreds of years antiquaries and archæologists dug and explored the valley, until it seemed impossible that anything new or unknown remained to be discovered. When the Earl of Carnarvon began his excavations the experts ridiculed the attempt and pronounced it futile; no undertaking seemed more hopeless. And yet, in the ruins and rubble that had been combed so often, Carnarvon found the entrance to the tomb of Tutankhamen, uncovered the fantastic riches of the treasure chamber, and made it possible to gain a wonderful insight into the customs of the rulers of Egypt more than three thousand years ago.

And so it is with Atlantis. The treasure within the legend has been buried under the rubble of misconceptions, follies and fantasies, the dead weight of prejudice and scepticism, and the ruins of wrong dating and faulty identifications that have accumulated around the legend in the two thousand five hundred years since Solon first heard it in Egypt. The ridicule of the experts falls upon any who try to dig beneath the debris of the centuries. But when the right path is found to the proper understanding of the legend, it leads to a treasure house that affords us a wide knowledge and a deep understanding of the life, thought, struggles and suffering of our ancestors more than three thousand years ago; it lays open to us one of the greatest and most momentous epochs in the history of the world.

The key to the proper understanding of the legend of Atlantis lies in the correct arrangement of the events it describes in their chronological sequence and according to their historical authenticity. This approach is followed in Section One (pp. 19–53). In Section Two (pp. 57–137) an attempt is made to reveal the hidden treasure of the legend; the geographical position of the Royal Isles, as well as the extent and organisation of the Atlantean kingdom, is established, and the authenticity of the information contained in the legend concerning the life and customs, culture and beliefs, and wealth and power of the Atlanteans is tested against our current knowledge of that age. In Section Three (pp. 141–207) will be found an account of what Homer, the greatest poet of all times, has written on Atlantis and of the legend this frequently trustworthy preserver of ancient history has handed down to us. Finally there is a report of the rediscovery of Atlantis in the summer of 1952 and a translation of Plato's account of Atlantis in the *Dialogues* of *Timæus* and of *Critias*.

Through all this we become acquainted with a people who

achieved greatness, suffered desperately, and yet still planned even greater things.

It is hoped that this contribution will encourage scholars in the relevant branches of the sciences to devote themselves afresh to the sadly neglected study of the legend of Atlantis. Their investigations would yield many riches and would go far to solve many hitherto unsolved problems of ancient history.

The Temple of Medinet Habu.

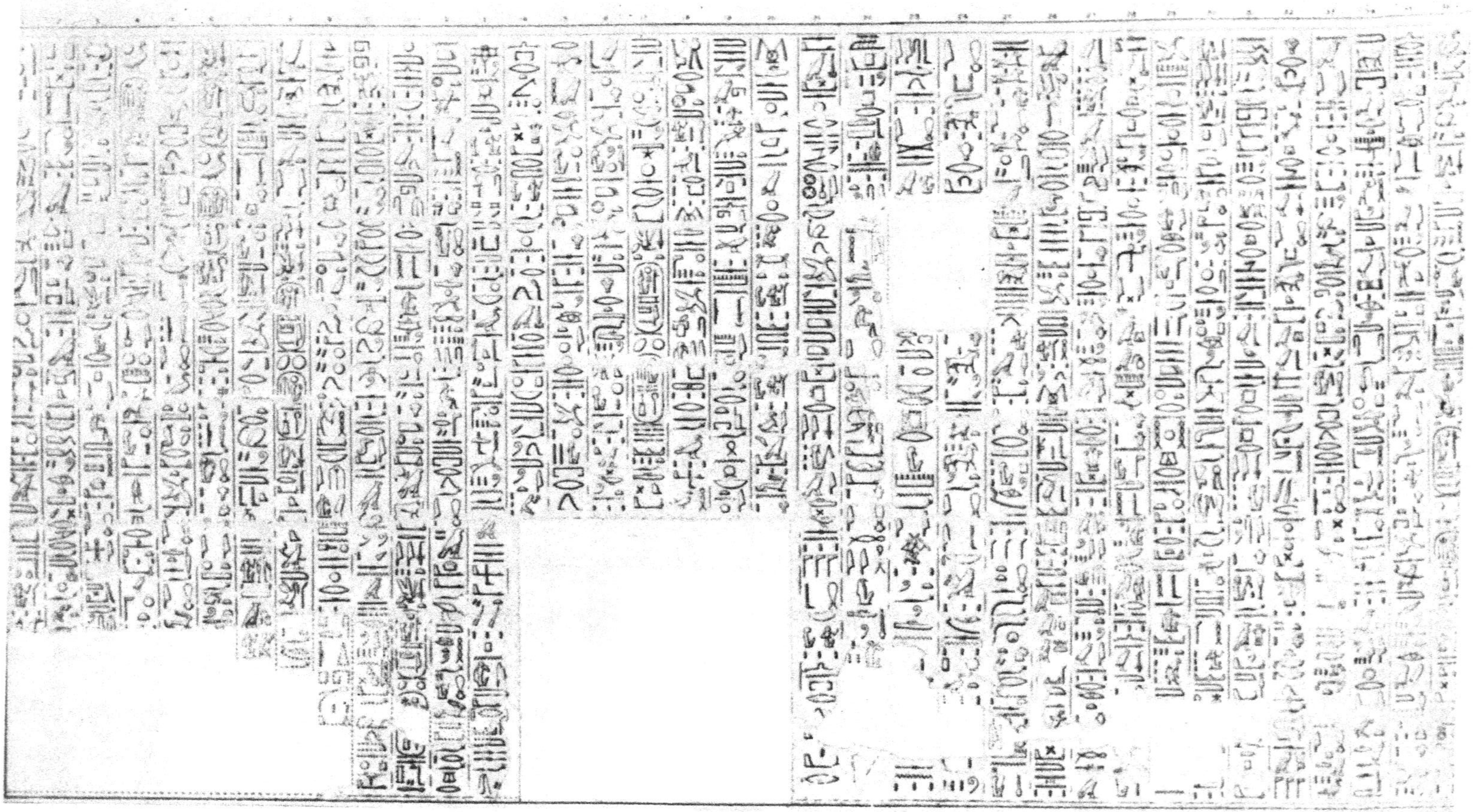

Wall inscriptions from the 5th year of Ramses III (1195 B.C.).

# SECTION ONE

# THE HISTORICAL BASIS
## OF THE ATLANTIS LEGEND

### I.  A SUMMARY OF THE LEGEND

PLATO, the great Greek philosopher and thinker (429–347 B.C.), has recorded for us the legend of Atlantis at two different places in his writings—in the *Dialogues* of *Timæus* and of *Critias*.  Of the origin and substance of the legend Plato tells us this:

Solon, legislator and one of the Seven Sages of Greece (640–559 B.C.), made a journey to Egypt to seek knowledge of ancient times.  He visited the city of Sais, whose priests had an unequalled reputation for their intimate knowledge of ancient history.  There he was received with great kindness and showered with honours.  The priests were only too happy to pass on to him the information they had extracted from their vast collection of papyri and ancient texts.

Solon was particularly impressed by a story of epic courage set in his own city of Athens; a story, he was told, that " although little known, was none the less true."  An old priest of Sais, basing his account on ancient Egyptian texts, told how a great army of people from Atlantis descended upon Europe and Asia Minor and united into one vast power all the territories that came under their domination.  These territories comprised " many islands and parts of the mainland by the Great Ocean in the North " and " the Mediterranean lands from Libya to Egypt and Europe to Tyrrhenia."  Through this combined power the King of the Atlantean peoples aimed at the domination of all the Greek and Egyptian territories and, in fact, of all the countries of the Mediterranean.  It was in repulsing this assault that the citizens of Athens proved their bravery and prowess. Athens placed herself at the head of the threatened Greek states, and eventually, as one state after another fell before the invaders, continued the fight alone and preserved her freedom. This heroic struggle also relieved the Egyptians, who were hard pressed by the invading armies, but were finally able to repulse the attacks of the Atlantean people.

The disorders and sufferings of those times were believed to have been caused by gigantic natural catastrophes of universal impact. The Egyptian priest reminded Solon of the Greek legend of Phæthon, son of Helios, god of the Sun, who entered his father's sun-chariot; unable to keep to his father's course, he burned or scorched many countries of the earth in the terrific heat of his passing. Eventually Zeus hurled Phæthon from the sky with a stroke of lightning and extinguished the great fires with floods and rainstorms.

The Egyptian priest in Sais admitted that the story sounded like a fable, but it did in fact contain a germ of truth; something very similar did happen in reality. Before that catastrophic age the earth's climate had been warm and fertile. The mountains of Greece were covered with a rich loam and lush forests; everywhere springs and rivers provided the land with abundant water. After the catastrophes the soil, which had been turned to dust by the intense heat, was swept away by the following floods, leaving only the skeleton of the country, the rocks and the stones. At the same time gigantic earthquakes and floods made the home of the Atlantean people uninhabitable. Atlantis, the royal isle of the Atlantean kingdom, is said to have been swallowed up by flood and earthquake in a single day and night of terror. Only a sea of mud remained in the place of the royal isle.

In the ensuing chapters of the Atlantis legend we are given detailed accounts of the exact position of the royal isle, the extent and power of the Atlantean kingdom and many other facts. We are told that on the royal isle, or Basileia, stood a castle of the kings of Atlantis and a temple dedicated to Poseidon, chief god of the Atlanteans. Here the Atlanteans are said to have found melted and solid copper, as well as a strange natural product known as orichalc; what this was the priest was unable to say. To us it is only a name, but the Atlanteans valued it as highly as gold. Apart from copper the Atlantic people worked with tin to a large extent. They also knew iron, but it was apparently not used during ceremonial festivities.

Many other details are known to us about Atlantis and the Atlanteans. According to Plato the Egyptian priest referred continually to ancient Egyptian papyri and inscriptions; we shall quote and discuss these details in the relevant chapters.

Solon had this story, which was originally translated from the Atlantis language into Egyptian, translated into Greek. He intended to write an epic poem based upon it, but the confusion he found in Athens on his return prevented him from completing this plan. The unfinished poem of the war between Athens and Atlantis, and the story of Atlantis itself, was handed down to Critias the Younger, who read it to a circle of friends in the presence of Socrates and Plato. Plato then wrote down the legend about ancient Athens and Atlantis, thus preserving it for posterity.

The Atlantis legend is, according to repeated assertions by Plato, the exact and faithful report of ancient Egyptian inscriptions and papyri collected by the priests in Sais and studied and told again by Solon. As Plato stressed, " the Atlantis legend is by no means a fairy-tale, but in every respect true history."

2. ATLANTIS—FABLE OR FACT?

Since the age of Plato, the legend of Atlantis has aroused the especial interest of countless people. " Fools and wise men, eccentrics and poets, philosophers and scientists, heretics and priests," said the Swedish oceanographer Petterson, have discussed the problem, whether Atlantis really existed or was only an ornament for Plato's theory of the state and social organisation—a model example invented to point a comparison between free democratic Athens and the all-powerful authoritarian state? This dispute whether the Atlantis legend was just a fairy-tale or a valuable historical record had already begun in Plato's time. He himself repeatedly asserted that the legend was no fairy-tale but completely true. Elsewhere he says that the Atlantis legend, although curious, is in every respect an historical certainty. Of the heroic deeds of the Athenians, who victoriously defended themselves against the attacking Atlantean soldiers, he remarked, " This brave act, although little known, none the less took place." In the *Dialogue* of *Critias*, Mnemosyne, the goddess of Remembrance, is invoked to ensure that all details are reported in accordance with the actual happenings.

Confident in the trustworthiness of Plato's beliefs, numerous scholars have attempted to solve the riddle of Atlantis. According to Ceram about twenty thousand books have been written since Plato's days on the subject; Braghine and Paul Herrman put the figure as high as twenty-five thousand. Using all possible means at the disposal of mankind, attempts were made to tear the veil from the secret. Societies were founded, conferences held, and research expeditions equipped in order to further the task. According to newspaper reports, in 1950 alone three large expeditions were trying to find Atlantis. Egerton Sykes believed the sunken isle to be in the neighbourhood of the Azores, more than 10,000 feet deep, and tried in vain to find traces of it, using radar equipment and depth charges. A descendant of Tolstoy is reported to have set off from the Bermudas because an American airman was said to have sighted walls and temple ruins in the South Atlantic during the last war. The Frenchman Henri Lhote equipped an expedition to the Sahara, where, in the waterless stone desert of Tanzerouft, he hoped to find the sunken island of Atlantis. The American scholar and politician Donelly called on the navies of the world, " instead of waging wars, to achieve useful cultural work by searching for the relics of Atlantis on the bed of the ocean."

When all these inquiries proved fruitless, the spiritualists and theosophists entered the field and proffered really fantastic solutions to the problem. Even bombs were used to settle the question. In August 1929, in a hall of the Sorbonne in Paris, two tear-gas bombs were thrown by a delegate at a congress of the Society for Atlantis Studies, in order to refute quickly, effectively and without further discussion the view of a speaker that Atlantis was to be identified with Corsica!

What has been the result of all this? Ceram has written that in spite of the twenty thousand volumes that have so far been published about Atlantis, no one has yet been able to prove its existence. It is small wonder, therefore, that many scholars believe the legend to be nothing but an illusion. Even Aristotle held this conviction, which has been strongly reinforced in our own time. The Swede Lindskog wrote that Atlantis was and is a legendary island, a creation of the imagination, nothing else. The Frenchman Abbé Moreux described the Atlantean legend as " pure fantasy," while the Austrian Rudolf Noll called it a Utopian romance lacking any historical background.

These judgments make it seem pointless to continue inquiring into the Atlantean legend. The verdict of science has been given; Plato has been accused of deliberate deception, all research concerning Atlantis condemned as a " contribution to the history of human folly," and all those who have treated the subject denounced as " fools," " Atlantomaniacs " and " eccentrics."

But the eternal sceptics who pronounced this severe judgment have made their task a little too easy. Not one of the many who have dismissed the Atlantean legend as pure fantasy has even attempted to prove his assertion. Plato has been denounced as a charlatan before his statements have even been tested, and his writings judged as " free poetry," without the question once being asked whether the papyri and inscriptions which he claimed as the basis for his report had not in fact existed or might not still be extant today.

### 3. SOLON WAS IN SAIS

Plato's opening statement was that Solon, in Sais, in Lower Egypt, saw for himself the inscriptions and papyri that embodied the Atlantean legend. The Egyptian priests, who collected and studied the texts, translated them from the ancient Egyptian and related them to Solon.

This assertion is repeated by Plato in many different forms. Brandenstein declares that Plato took the greatest trouble to verify the reliability of the Atlantean legend. To authenticate it, Plato tells how the Egyptian priests acquired the papyri, how Solon wrote down the story, intending to use it as the basis for a poem, and how the chaos he found upon his return to Athens prevented him from completing the undertaking. Plato declares, moreover, that the legend had originally been translated from the Atlantis language into Egyptian and was only for Solon translated again into Greek, and he adds that there were numerous proofs of its correctness. It eventually reached Plato through various intermediaries.

Should not we also verify these statements?

There is no doubt that Solon really did go to Egypt; the fact has been confirmed by many ancient writers and chroniclers. He began his ten-year journey, after he had given Athens his fruitful laws, in order to collect information about prehistoric times. His first goal was Sais, the residence of the Pharaohs, because its priests had gathered and studied the ancient inscriptions and texts of their country and had an intimate knowledge of ancient history.

There is no doubt that this is correct. When Solon travelled to ancient Egypt, Sais, situated at the mouth of the Nile, would logically be the city to visit first. It was also, in fact, the residence of the Pharaohs, and Psamtik I (663–609 B.C.) had allowed a colony of Greek merchants to whom he had granted special privileges to settle in the neighbourhood of the royal residence. In Solon's time the Pharaoh Ahmose II (570–525 B.C.), mentioned by Plato, reigned in Sais; he favoured the Greeks to such an extent as to arouse the jealousy of the Egyptians. Solon had acquired from Ahmose several laws, for example that " every year each inhabitant has to show the governor by what means he earns his livelihood." We have further to believe Plato when he says that Solon had been to Sais, that he was received well and showered with honours.

Did the priests in Sais really collect and study in detail historical texts, inscriptions and papyri, as Plato tells us in the *Dialogues*? Again we must confirm Plato. The intensive study of the past was in fact the main occupation of the priests of Sais in those days. Breasted, the great authority on Egyptian history, says of the priests in Sais, in another connection: The writings and sacred rolls of past centuries were searched for with great zeal, and with the dust of the ages which covered them they were collected, sorted out and arranged. Such a classical education led the priests back into a long-forgotten world, whose inherited wisdom, as with the Chinese and Mohammedans, formed the highest moral laws. The world had grown old, and with particular pleasure they occupied themselves with its long-bygone youth. The age of the Sais, with its continuous reference to past conditions, has rightly been called an age of restoration.

Thus Plato's statement that the priests in Sais collected and studied ancient documents is confirmed by one of the greatest authorities on Egyptian history.

Were there in Sais, as Plato maintained, texts and inscriptions, or copies of them, that reported the great war of the Atlantis people, the terrible natural catastrophes of the age, and the deliverance of Egypt from the onslaught of the Atlantean warriors? Proclus, a commentator on Plato, reports that the priests in Sais showed the same inscriptions and papyri to Crantor of Soli (330–270 B.C.), who wrote the first commentary on Timæus. They did in fact exist, and the question arises whether these inscriptions—or at least some of them, for countless ancient Egyptian texts have been lost in the course of the centuries—are still in existence today.

4. THE DATING OF THE EVENTS DESCRIBED IN THE ATLANTIS
LEGEND

Before we begin the attempt to trace the ancient text that describes the events reported by Plato we must first fix the dating of the events themselves. Upon our solution of this problem—the most important of all in the study of Atlantis—depends our verdict on the authenticity of the legend; the whole story stands or falls by our answer.

It is rather strange that hardly any scholar has inquired

into the question of dating or thought it worth while to go into it more deeply. The problem of where Atlantis was situated has taken precedence over the question of when it was destroyed. The few scholars who have dealt with the dating have, in spite of the means at our disposal today for the solution of such problems, given really ridiculous answers; the events described to Solon have been placed in almost every ten thousand years between 1000000 B.C. and 500 B.C. If these are the results of modern scholars it is not surprising to find that Plato's own dating—eight thousand years before Solon—is completely impossible, or, as Knotel rightly says, complete nonsense. Many of the things mentioned in detail in the Atlantean legend—amongst others, the Greek states, the city of Athens, an Egyptian empire, copper, tin, the first iron, and chariots—certainly did not exist eight thousand years before Solon, that is in 8600 B.C. There must be a mistake here, perhaps an error in translation; we cannot accept this dating.

But fortunately, in addition to this mis-statement, the legend contains many allusions that enable us to date the events correctly. There is, for instance, the frequent remark that the Atlanteans had a great wealth of copper and tin, and were even the earliest users of iron.

A race which possessed copper and tin did in fact live during the Bronze Age, from about 2000 to 1000 B.C. If, as has been said, iron tools were already known in Atlantis, then the island must have been in existence at the end of the Bronze Age, at the time when iron first appeared.

The question of the use of the first iron tools or implements has been closely investigated by the well-known authority on prehistoric metallurgy, Wilhelm Witter. Witter's exhaustive examination of archæological finds led him to the definite conclusion that the first iron implements made by human hands came in with the invasion of the sea peoples from the North, who swept down like a hurricane upon the Mediterranean countries towards the end of the thirteenth century B.C. According to Witter, at least some of the North people must have mastered techniques of iron before they began their great migration.

If, as Plato maintains, the legend of Atlantis is in every aspect an historically accurate and valuable report, then the events he describes must have taken place towards the end of the thirteenth century, at the time of the introduction of iron, when copper and tin were still largely used.

Perhaps Olaf Rudbeck (1630–1703) was right in assuming that there had been an error in translation, that we must think not of eight thousand years but of eight thousand months between the fall of Atlantis and Solon's stay in Egypt. If this is so, the fall of Atlantis must have taken place about 1200 B.C.

This assumption of the Swedish historian leads us to the exact time when Atlantis must have perished. The Egyptian year was of twelve months, and eight thousand " months " are therefore 666 years. If we subtract these 666 years from the date of Solon's stay in Egypt—560 B.C.—we arrive at the year 1226 B.C., and this year was perhaps that of the beginning of the Atlantean catastrophe. It was in this year that Libyans, driven from their homes by terrible natural disasters, attacked the Pharaoh Merneptah; in almost exactly 1200 B.C. the people of the Northern Mediterranean reached Greece, arriving at the Egyptian border in 1195 B.C. We can easily imagine that the North people—like the Cymbrians and Teutons a thousand years later—were on the move for twenty to thirty years, until they were finally stopped by Ramses III in 1195 B.C.

There is, in fact, much to be said for Rudbeck's belief that Solon misunderstood the Egyptian priests, and that the beginning of the catastrophes and wars described in the Atlantis legend has to be put at eight thousand months before Solon.

Rudbeck and many other scholars after him have pointed out that the lengthy life-spans recorded in Genesis v. are the result of the same confusion between the ancient oriental reckoning by months and the more modern reckoning by years. All the ages given have therefore to be divided by twelve. In this way Adam was not 930 but 77 years, Seth not 912 but 76 years, Mahalaleel not 895 but 74 years, Jared not 962 but 80 years, Methuselah not 969 but 81, and

Lamech not 777 but 64. Even today the Egyptians reckon time by months. King Farouk writes in his memoirs: " Our calendar is counted by months, and not like the Gregorian calendar in most Western countries by a year of 365 days."

## 5. CONTEMPORARY TEXTS AND INSCRIPTIONS RELATING TO THE LEGEND

We raised the question earlier whether some of the texts to which the priests in Sais referred, and which were seen by Solon and Crantor, might not be extant today.

We have established that all the events described in the Atlantis legend must have taken place at the time of the earliest use of iron, at the end of the thirteenth century B.C., and it remains to discover whether there exist any inscriptions and papyri of this time to confirm the statements of the legend.

In fact quite a number of such texts are known:

1. Inscriptions from about the time of the Pharaoh Merneptah (1232–1214 B.C.), among them the great Tablet of Karnak and the Stele of Athribis.

2. The inscriptions and wall pictures in the temple of Ramses III (1200–1168 B.C.) in Medinet Habu, where thousands of square yards of historical inscriptions and reliefs are carved in the walls and columns.

3. The Papyrus Harris, the most comprehensive text preserved for us from the ancient Orient. It is a papyrus roll one hundred feet long upon which is written a kind of Government report of Ramses III.

4. The Papyrus Ipuwer, in which an eye-witness of terrible catastrophes in Egypt complains vehemently that these misfortunes were brought about by the Pharaoh. The Papyrus Ipuwer has been dated by Erman at about 2500 B.C., but that date is wrong. The papyrus mentions bronze and so can only have originated during the Bronze Age, which in Egypt as elsewhere lasted from about 2000 to 1000 B.C. It alludes also to the " Land of the Keftyew," which did not appear until after the eighteenth dynasty, 1580–1350 B.C. Furthermore, its description of the natural catastrophes and of the invasion of strange races into the Nile delta agrees to a

large extent with those of Medinet Habu and the Papyrus Harris, which proves that the Papyrus Ipuwer originated at the same time as these texts, that is, about 1200 B.C.

5. Old Testament sources, particularly Exodus, will also have to be consulted. They contain what can be shown by comparison with the other original texts to be faithful descriptions of that age.

Exodus describes the emigration of the Children of Israel from Egypt and the terrible plagues which made it possible. This event took place between 1232 and 1200 B.C. In Exodus i. 11 it is reported that the Children of Israel were forced during their slavery to build the towns of Pithom and Ramses as places of storage. Both these towns were built by Ramses II (1298—1232 B.C.). Pithom in the Wadi Tumilat, which is the natural gateway into Egypt from Asia, was built as a fortress town, while Ramses, or " the House of Ramses," was built in the Nile delta as a new residence for the Pharaoh after whom it was named. This same Ramses II, builder of Pithom and Ramses, was also the Hebrew " Pharaoh of oppression."

According to Exodus ii. 23, this Pharaoh died before the emigration of the Israelites and the outbreak of the great afflictions known as the " ten plagues of Egypt." The Pharaoh at the time of the Exodus must therefore have been a successor of Ramses II. But when Ramses III ascended to the throne in the year 1200 B.C. Egypt was already in a state of complete devastation. The natural catastrophes described in Exodus must therefore have taken place between 1232 and 1200 B.C.; today they are usually assumed to have begun in about 1220 B.C., which seems to be correct.

Exodus, then, records the same disasters as those described in the other inscriptions and papyri listed above and in the Atlantis legend.

6. We have to add to these contemporary sources much additional information handed down to us by ancient poets and writers of a later age. As this information cannot safely be dated we shall quote it only in exceptional cases.

7. In addition there is much archæological evidence which, taken together with the numerous findings of natural

science, impressively confirms the statements of contemporary inscriptions and of the Atlantis legend.

## 6. THE NATURAL CATASTROPHES OF ABOUT 1200 B.C.

The critics' chief objections to the Atlantis legend have always been aimed at Plato's account of the extensive natural catastrophes said to have afflicted the whole world at the time of the fall of Atlantis, and to have caused the great wars of the Atlantean people. This report has been branded as a " pure invention " by Plato in an attempt to make his " cosmological speculation " more plausible. That such a suspicion should arise is easily understandable, for Plato tells of catastrophes so unequalled that their dismissal as pure invention seems only too justifiable.

According to Plato, the priests of Sais told Solon that at that time the earth was parched and scorched to an extent that defeats imagination; great fires destroyed many lands and forests, earthquakes shook the world and wrought enormous destruction, many springs and rivers dried up, and the royal isle of Atlantis was engulfed by the sea. Finally great floods and rainstorms added to the chaos. Thus, in a fantastic whirl of terrible catastrophes, an unusually favourable and fruitful age was followed by one with a much more severe and barren climate.

Do these statements correspond with the facts? Did the turn of the thirteenth century B.C. suffer such universal disaster or are the critics right who accuse Plato of romanticising?

(a) *The desiccation and the great fire*

The contemporary documents declare with certainty that such catastrophes did in fact occur towards the end of the thirteenth century B.C. One source says of the desiccation and the great fire: " A terrible torch hurled flames from the sky to seek the souls of Libyans and to destroy their tribe." Edgerton explains that lightning from the sky had afflicted the Libyans and destroyed their tribe. Similar details may be found elsewhere. " The heat burned like a flame on their land. Their bones burned and melted in their limbs."

" The heat in their land burned like a fire in an oven."
And, concerning the North people: " Their forests and
people were destroyed by the fire." " Before them spread a
sea of flames." Repeatedly we find it recorded that the
enemies of Egypt were burned or afflicted by the great fire.
But Egypt also suffered. An eye-witness has reported that
walls, gates and columns were destroyed by flames, the sky
was in chaos, no fruit or food could be found, in a single day
everything was destroyed and the land left to dry out like
cut flax.

In Exodus we read: " The Lord sent thunder and hail and
the fire ran along upon the ground, and the Lord rained hail
upon the land of Egypt. So there was hail, and fire mingled
with the hail, very grievous, such as there was none like it in
all the land of Egypt since it became a nation."

Ovid wrote in *Metamorphoses*, in all probability basing his
account on reliable ancient sources: " The earth was alight,
mountains were raised, great gaps appeared, the rivers dried
up; great towns vanished with all their inhabitants and
enormous outbreaks of fires turned human beings into ashes."
Every phrase of this description can be confirmed by contemporary or other historical sources.

It is certainly true that in the last decades of the thirteenth
century B.C. Libya became a desert. During the Bronze Age
it was, like large tracts of the Sahara, a fertile land with
plenty of water. Countless rock drawings of herds of cattle,
horse-drawn carts, fishes and ships have been found in places
where today not even a camel could survive. Numerous
graveyards dating back to the early Stone and Bronze Ages
and other archæological finds prove that the country was
once populous and highly fertile. But in about 1200 B.C.
Libya became parched, and its people sought refuge in the
Nile delta. The old priest of Sais who told Solon of these
catastrophes was probably correct in saying, " In those days
it was the Nile that saved our country." For while the rivers
and lakes of Libya, fed from the Central and Southern
Sahara, dried up, the Nile continued to flow through the
melting of the glaciers in the 15,000-feet mountains where it
had its source.

But the most impressive proof of the catastrophic desiccation of about 1200 B.C. comes from the misnamed lake-dwellings of Europe. Remains of settlements have been found in many European lakes and rivers, although often a considerable distance from the shore. They date from the period between 2000 and 1200 B.C. Until recently it was believed that these were the remains of lake-dwellings, that is of houses built on stilts rising out of the water. But as our knowledge of prehistoric settlement was increased by archæological excavations the riddle of these lake-dwellings became more puzzling. There seemed no purpose in building such an extraordinary kind of settlement in our European climate. The German scholar O. Paret attacked this problem from a new angle and found a number of technical objections to the explanations that had previously been offered. He came to the conclusion that the lake-dwellings whose posts were found in the lakes, rivers and swamps of Europe were in fact not lake-dwellings at all, but settlements built on firm ground. That being so, the fact that these remains were found far out in the waters could only mean that at the time of their erection the water level was about fifteen feet lower than it is today. All these settlements had been built at the edge of the waters during the time of drought and had been inundated and evacuated when the lakes and rivers rose again. Since this applies to all lake-dwellings throughout Central and Northern Europe the cause must have been a general and not a local one—a climatic catastrophe beginning with extensive drought and ending in tremendous floods. The name lake-dwellings was a romantic error and widespread natural disasters must be regarded as historically proven facts.

These lake-dwellings have been found to date only from the time of the two great ages of drought in about 2000 and 1200 B.C. Paret was able to ascertain that the drought of 1200 B.C. was much more severe and widespread than that of 2000 B.C. To illustrate the events of that age he reminds us, like the priest of Sais 2,520 years before him, of the beautiful Greek legend of Phæthon, who drove his father's sun-chariot along the wrong paths and burned many countries until Zeus

**THEN**

Fence | Waste pit | Burnt-down house | Fence | former (more normal) water-level

Moraine gravel

Occupation of the beach during the dry period

**NOW**

former beach

after destruction of village by the rising waters

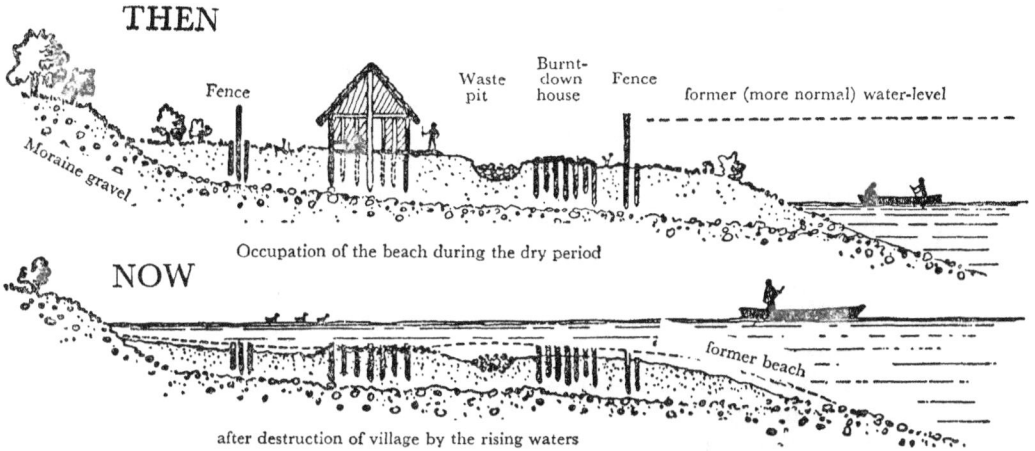

Sections through a lakeside village from the dry period around 1200 B.C. showing how the present-day remains gave rise to the mistaken theory of " lake-dwellings."

extinguished the flames with great rainstorms and floods. This legend seems also to Paret a good illustration for the natural catastrophes of about 1200 B.C. This climatic reverse resulted in so great a food shortage amongst the races of the world that it forced many of them to become cannibals. It was instrumental in the movement of races in Middle and Southern Europe; it overthrew the old world and created the basis for a new one. It was the cause of the flood which determined the destiny of the world.

All these observations and the contemporary inscriptions quoted above leave no doubt that the great drought reported in the Atlantis legend and the " great fire " did in fact take place at the time claimed, that is, towards the end of the thirteenth century B.C. On this point too Plato's story is not pure invention but in every respect true history.

(b) *Earthquakes and floods*

The same applies to the " gigantic earthquakes and floods " reported by Plato, which have also been described as a product of the great Greek's imagination. In support of them also countless contemporary reports and scientific proofs can be quoted.

3—A

The inscriptions in Medinet Habu record that the North peoples' country was destroyed, and " their soul exposed to mortal danger." Egypt lay in complete desolation, its towns destroyed and its inhabitants victims of the frightful catastrophe of Nature. Eusebius, Bishop of Cæsarea, reports, on the basis of ancient writings of Exodus: " There was hail and earthquake, and those who fled from the hail into the houses were killed by the earthquake, which caused all the houses and most of the temples to collapse."

Tacitus (*Annals*, iv, 55) says: " The people of Halikatnass assure me that there has not been an earthquake in their country for twelve hundred years." Diodorus of Sicily, who lived shortly before Christ, wrote in his universal history that twelve hundred years before him Lake Tritonis in North Africa disappeared in a terrible earthquake. Justinus the Martyr (d. A.D. 165) reports of the Phœnicians, who advanced from the east to the coast of the Mediterranean at the end of the thirteenth century B.C., that they were driven by great earthquakes from their original home of Assyria.

Simultaneously with these earthquakes there are said to have been storms so terrible that, according to Ramses III, the islands of the North people were " uprooted by the storm and swept away." The hieroglyphic inscription of El Arish, which describes the same disasters, says: " The country was in great distress, misfortune fell upon the earth and there was a tremendous tumult in the capital. For nine days no one could leave the palace. During these nine days there was such a storm that neither men nor gods [by which are probably meant the royal family] could see the faces around them."

The storm is also mentioned in Exodus, which relates that it sprang from the east and then changed to the west: " And the Lord turned a mighty strong west wind."

The simultaneous occurrence of powerful, westerly winds and gigantic earthquakes caused floods and landslides. Ramses III reported that the Delta flooded its coasts. In Exodus it is said of this: " Thou didst blow with thy wind, the sea covered them [the Egyptians]: they sank as lead in the mighty waters."

In many parts of Greece there are reminders of the Deucalionic flood, which Greek writers dated at the same time as the fire of Phæthon. Eusebius wrote that the flood of Deucalion, the fire of Phæthon and the Israelite exodus from Egypt all took place at the same time, and Augustinus thought the flood of Deucalion contemporary with Moses' exodus from Egypt. It is also very likely that the numerous Greek myths dealing with the Deucalionic flood are a reminder of the gigantic floods and rainstorms around 1200 B.C. In Delphi, in the mouth of Anthesterion, special sacrifices were offered to Apollo in gratitude for his safe delivery of the people's ancestors from the Deucalionic flood.

We have already seen that from the evidence of the so-called lake-dwellings the catastrophic effects of the rapidly rising water level of the lakes and rivers can easily be proved. "As the lake-dwellings suddenly stop at Lake Constance and the Swiss lakes the reason must be found in a far wider cause," says Paret. The "far wider cause," according to him, was the great climatic change at the beginning of the Iron Age, which led to a rapid rise of the water level of the lakes and rivers and the flooding of the "lake-dwellings." These lake-dwellings of the period around 1200 B.C. are visible proof that the gigantic rainstorms and floods described in the Atlantis legend did in fact follow the drought age of the second half of the thirteenth century B.C. Paret assures us that the climatic catastrophes of that age were seen "in the right perspective" by Plato.

In the moors of Northern Germany, Jonas has found many traces of a well-defined "damp zone" which he dates on the basis of archæological finds to 1200 B.C. According to him the great majority of moor and humus growth has grown on the dry soil of the previous ages after a new wave of floods in the time around 1100–1000 B.C.

At this same time the great changes on the west coast of the Cimbrian peninsula must have taken place. The North Sea, which until then stretched only as far as Heligoland, overwhelmed wide stretches of land and reached what is known as the "Middleback." The dry land jutting out into the sea was torn away and cliffs were formed. At other places

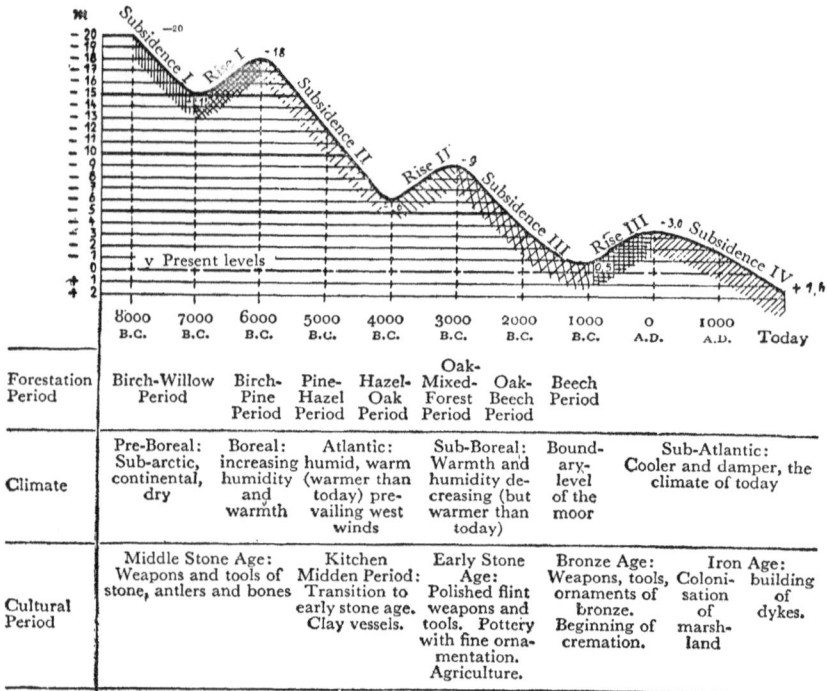

Diagram of land subsidence in the southern North Sea area. Subsidence III and the boundary level of the moor (= the natural catastrophes of 1200 B.C.) coincide.

gigantic " beach walls " were thrown up by the waves; in this way were created the " Doons " at Marne and the " Lundner Nehrung," a long and narrow tongue of land twelve miles long and five miles wide.

These cliffs and beach walls could not have been formed earlier. Ernst Beckman, who studied this stretch of the coast in detail, put the date of their formation " around the turn of the Bronze Age or the Iron Age." We shall see later that before the catastrophes there existed a large island situated to the west of the Holstein coast, in the neighbourhood of Heligoland. This island acted as a breakwater to the Holstein west coast and would have effectively protected it from the terrible devastations revealed by the cliffs and beach walls. Only after the island had submerged was it possible for the sea to destroy a large part of the coast.

That the cliffs and beach walls did not exist in the Bronze Age is proved by the complete absence of archæological finds of the period in this area, although they are numerous in the immediate vicinity of the " Middleback." Finds dating from the Iron Age, on the other hand, show that the beach walls did exist then, so they must have been formed in the catastrophes of about 1200 B.C.

The Greeks kept this catastrophe alive in their folk memory. Phæthon, when Zeus threw him from the sky by lightning, crashed down at the mouth of the Eridanus, where his body was found and buried by his sisters, the Heliades. The sisters were changed into poplars and, standing at the shore of the Eridanus, wept over their brother. Their tears are said to have fallen into the river and turned into amber, which was washed ashore on the island of Basileia in the North Sea.

It is therefore of no importance whether we follow Richard Henning, the author of many works on historical and geographical problems, in identifying the Eridanus with the Elbe, or the German scholar and writer Heinar Schilling and the Swedish historian Sven Nilsson, in identifying it with the Eider, because the mouth of both rivers lay in those times in the vicinity of Heligoland. Contemporary ancient Egyptian texts add to the evidence of the cliffs and beach walls to show that a terrible natural catastrophe must have taken place in about 1200 B.C.

In conclusion we can say that all the information given in the Atlantis legend about the world-wide natural catastrophes of 1200 B.C. has been confirmed to the fullest extent by numerous contemporary inscriptions, by archæological observations and scientific investigations, and by countless more recent stories, only a very few of which we have quoted. When we compare the accounts of contemporary inscriptions with the stories of Plato we have to admit that Plato has told of these catastrophes in a factual, if not reticent manner. They were of much greater consequence than Plato's report leads us to believe. They marked the end of the climatically favourable Bronze Age, they ushered in a new, difficult age, the Iron Age, and caused the floods which determined the destiny of the world.

### 7. THE MILITARY EXPEDITIONS OF THE ATLANTIS PEOPLE

The military expeditions of the Atlantis people against Egypt and Greece, reported by Plato, have so far without exception been discounted as legend, in the same way as the natural catastrophes. Even scholars like Adolf Schulten and Wilhelm Brandenstein, who believe in the " historical substance " of the Atlantis legend, have tried to dismiss the expeditions of the Atlantis people as " figments of the imagination." Our ideas of power relations in the Bronze Age make it seem incomprehensible that in those days a tribe existed which could cross Europe and Asia Minor and reach the Egyptian border, with the aim of dominating Greece, Egypt and all the land within the straits. The conception of uniting Europe and the Mediterranean countries under one power is so modern that it seems astonishing even as a flight of fancy by Plato, but that it should have been conceived nearly one thousand years before Plato and almost translated into reality is quite unthinkable to the modern mind. This part of the Atlantis legend has accordingly been unhesitatingly dismissed and even used as proof of the historical worthlessness of Plato's whole account.

But here also contemporary inscriptions and papyri disprove the hasty judgments of the sceptic. We shall compare Plato's account of this military campaign and of the " Pan-European " plan of the Atlanteans with contemporary documents and show that here also he added nothing, and kept strictly to the ancient Egyptian texts brought back by Solon.

The main points of Plato's account of the great military expedition are these:

1. The peoples of the Atlantean kingdom united into one force and resolved upon a single war expedition to dominate Greece and Egypt, as well as all the land within the straits.

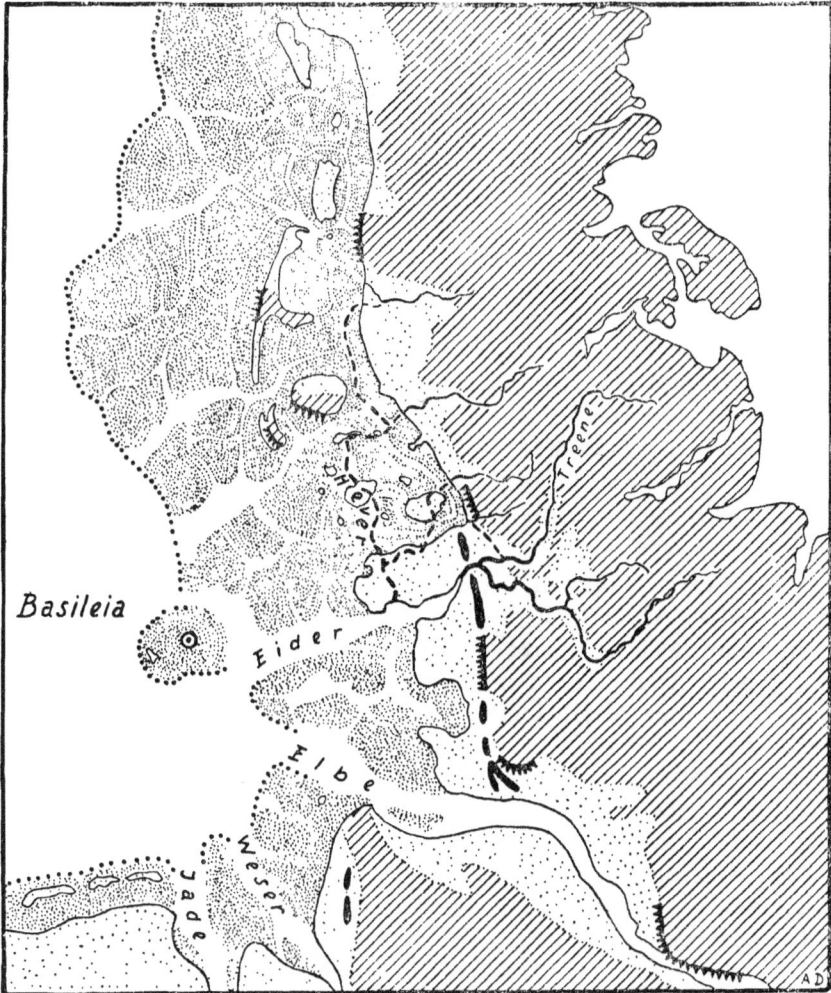

| present coastline | | coastal embankment |
| coastline after 1200 B.C. | | former course of river |
| 20m. depth contour | | land destroyed |
| cliff formation | | in 1200 B.C. |

The extent of the catastrophe of 1200 B.C. The sea inundated the island and mainland area between the present 20 metres depth contour and the " Middle-back " of Schleswig-Holstein and created coastal embankments and cliffs there.

2. In the course of the expedition the Atlantis people wandered through Europe and subjected the whole of Greece with the exception of Athens. They then invaded Asia Minor and penetrated to the border of Egypt, which they threatened but were unable to conquer.

3. Of the Mediterranean countries, Libya, Greece and Europe as far as the Tyrrhenian Sea came under the rule of the Atlantean kings. These countries then joined the great expedition.

4. A large, well-equipped and highly organised army, strong in war chariots, and a powerful fleet were at the disposal of the Atlantis power. Ten kings, known as " the Ten," commanded the forces under the supreme command of the King of Atlantis.

5. The expedition of the Atlantis people took place in the time of the great natural catastrophes. According to results so far obtained this great expedition must then have set out in about 1200 B.C.

It is certain that in the decades around 1200 B.C. events took place which confirm the account of the Atlantis legend to an astonishing degree.

These events have gone into history under the names of " The Great Migration," " Dorian Migration," " Ægean Migration," " Illyrian Migration." They have also been named, after the races which played a decisive rôle in the initial stages of the Great Migration, " Military expeditions of the North and Sea peoples."

Apart from the contemporary inscriptions we have already discussed—which were described by Bilabel as " documents of the greatest historical value "—the results of numerous archæological excavations help to throw light on this decisive epoch of European history, and enable us to reconstruct the course of events.

### The expedition against Egypt

During the reign of the Pharaoh Merneptah the Libyans and their allies broke into Egypt from the west, compelled by the parching of their country to leave their homeland to seek food in Egypt. They were accompanied by the Libyan women and children. Under the leadership of King Meryey the Libyans succeeded in advancing as far as Memphis and Heliopolis, where they settled.

In the fifth year of his reign, 1227 B.C., Merneptah resolved to drive out the invaders, and on the 3rd of Epiphi (April) the battle of Perire was fought. After six hours the Libyans were defeated and took to flight. Rich booty fell into the hands of the victorious Pharaoh, including 9,111 bronze swords, three to four feet long. The number of dead left on the battlefield amounted to 6,359 Libyans, 2,370 North people, 222 Shekclesh (Sicilians) and 742 Etruscans.

But although the united Libyans and North people suffered a serious defeat, they rose again. The battle of Perire was only the beginning of a series of much bigger and bloodier events, only an overture to a world revolution of unparalleled extent.

We can now see by the measures the Eastern Mediterranean countries took that they saw a terrible storm approaching. Towards the end of the thirteenth century B.C. the Athenians erected the great cyclopic fortresses and armed for their defence. In Mycenæ the fortifications were strengthened and at the same time care was taken that the water supply to the fortress was well secured. The fortress of Tiryns was built and all fortifications were strengthened.

In Asia Minor the Hittite Kings attempted by strongly fortifying their capital Boghazköi and by concluding a military pact with Egypt to forestall the day of judgment. The Pharaohs brought their country to a high pitch of readiness by a great rearmament programme, by rebuilding the towns destroyed by the catastrophes, and by raising vast armies of mercenaries.

In about 1200 B.C. the threatened storm broke loose. From the north great armies invaded and occupied the whole of Greece; only Athens withstood the attack. The invading North people came by land, but they must have been experienced shipbuilders and skilful sailors. According to legend they built a powerful fleet at Naupactos on the Gulf of Corinth, crossed the Peloponnese and destroyed the

powerful Achäic and Cretan fleets. They then occupied
Crete, the Ægean islands and Cyprus.

It is possible that a large force of the North people had
already turned aside from Greece, crossed the Bosphorus,
and destroyed Troy, the Troy of Homer, which had been
already destroyed eighty years before by the Mycenean
Greeks. A long trail of destruction marked the course of
these tribes which had followed the land route, operating
apparently hand in hand with those which had crossed the
sea to Greece and Cyprus.

Asia Minor was now occupied and crossed, the mighty land
of the Hittites was destroyed and disappeared almost from
the face of the earth. Excavations show that Boghazköi,
the Hittite capital was plundered and destroyed in spite of
its splendid fortifications.

The contemporary Egyptian inscriptions confirm the
results of the excavations and describe the subsequent course
of these great military expeditions. Ramses III reports:
" The North people have made a conspiracy on their
island. The islands have been torn away and have gone with
the wind. The lands of the Hittite, Codes, Carcemish,
Arzawa, Alasia [Cyprus] were destroyed. They erected their
camp at a place in Amor [Southern Syria]. They destroyed
the country and its inhabitants as if they had never existed."

Apparently the North people came together in their camp
at Amor for the decisive attack against Egypt.

Ramses III ordered general mobilisation. He fortified his
border in the north, secured the harbours, and assembled
battleships of all kinds, strongly armed, and manned from
bow to stern. He ordered arms to equip auxiliary troops.
Recruiting and equipment were directed by the Crown
Prince. Apart from native troops, negroes and soldiers from
Sardinia were also enlisted. It was said of this army that the
soldiers were the best in Egypt—they were like " lions
roaring on the mountains."

In the fifth year of Ramses' reign (1195 B.C.), after some
seemingly weak attacks, a full-scale attack was made on
Egypt, probably based on a unified plan. The Libyans, once
again united with the North peoples, attempted to gain a

foothold near the mouth of the Nile, and the main force of the enemy set out from Amor towards Egypt. Ramses III and his troops moved towards the enemy.

The ensuing battle was destined to be of world historical importance. By good fortune and the skilful deployment of his forces Ramses III was able to withstand the onslaught. Hundreds of thousands of the Northerners were slain or captured. Their warships, some of which had already reached the coast, found themselves facing a wall of metal. They were encircled by Egyptian troops armed with spears, driven on to dry land and surrounded. There was such slaughter of the ships that corpses covered them from stern to bow. Many of the Northern ships capsized and their crews drowned. The North people attacking by land were encircled and the women and children they had brought with them in their clumsy ox-carts were killed or carried off into slavery.

An attack by Egyptian soldiers and allies on a wagon-train of the North Sea peoples containing women and children.

Wrescinski, the well-known Egyptologist, believes that the outcome of the war was decided in the sea battle, because it was this that was described in the greatest detail. The wall pictures in the Medinet Habu show clearly how the North people were defeated in spite of their superior seamanship. Their ships had no oars and relied upon sails for their propulsion, but on this fateful day there was apparently no wind, and for this reason the sails were fixed, the rudders left unmanned and the ships drifted aimlessly off the coast. The ships' crews were armed only with swords and spears, that is, only for close fighting, and there were no archers among them. The Egyptians, on the other hand, emerged from the river mouth in fast ships, driven by many oars. They carried bows and arrows and were able to encircle and dispose of the clumsy ships from a safe distance. Their oarsmen and archers fired from behind bulwarks made up of the bodies of Northerners captured and lashed to the ships. When the crews of the enemy ships were reduced in numbers by the arrows of the Egyptians the Egyptian warships approached, threw grappling-irons into the open sails of the Northern ships, and capsized them. Their crews leaped into the water, where most were killed, only a few reaching the coast.

The reliefs at Medinet Habu have preserved for us touching scenes of the North people's heroic struggle. On one ship, crowded with fallen Northerners, a few men still continue the hopeless battle; on another a Northern warrior supports a seriously wounded comrade with his right arm and raises a protecting shield with his left. On a third ship the Northerners, themselves threatened by death, are trying to save the wounded floating in the water. Similar scenes of the highest comradeship and death-defying courage of the North people are shown in the great relief of the land battle. Otto Eisfeld, who has closely studied the age of the Philistines and Phœnicians, is undoubtedly right in saying: " The Egyptian descriptions of the battles of Ramses III against the Philistines show to a remarkable degree the death-defying courage of the Philistines." (The Philistines were the leading people of the Northern and sea peoples' coalition.)

The hands of the Northerners killed or wounded in the land and sea battles were cut off, thrown on to a heap and counted. In this way the exact number of casualties was determined. For earlier battles the number of hands cut from the fallen enemy had been precisely counted. For example, after the battle near the Libyan border between Ramses III and the combined Libyan and Northern forces 25,215 hands had been counted. But nowhere are we told the number of hands resulting from the decisive battles of 1195 B.C., only that they were countless in number, and the prisoners taken

An Egyptian warship in action against a ship of the North Sea peoples.
From the Sea Battle Relief in Medinet Habu.

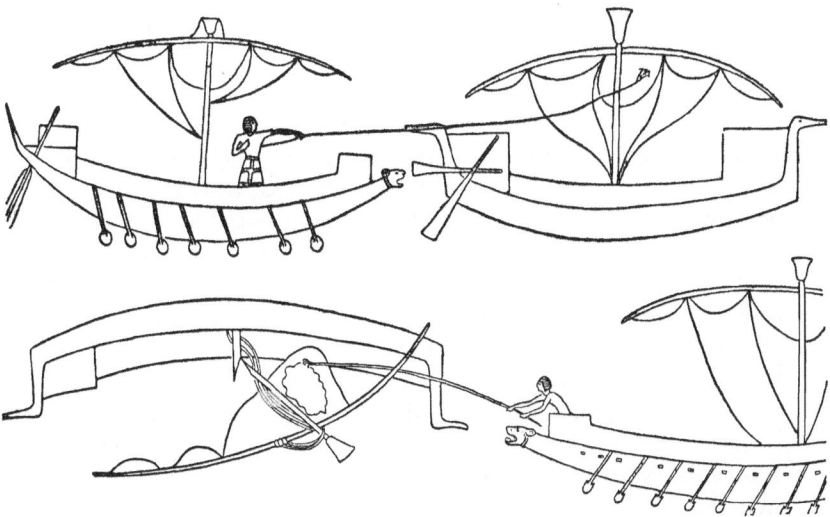

How the ships of the North Sea Peoples were made to capsize (Medinet Habu).

as numerous as the sands by the sea. We can assume that indefinite expressions were chosen because the number of the fallen or wounded enemy was far greater than that of previous battles.

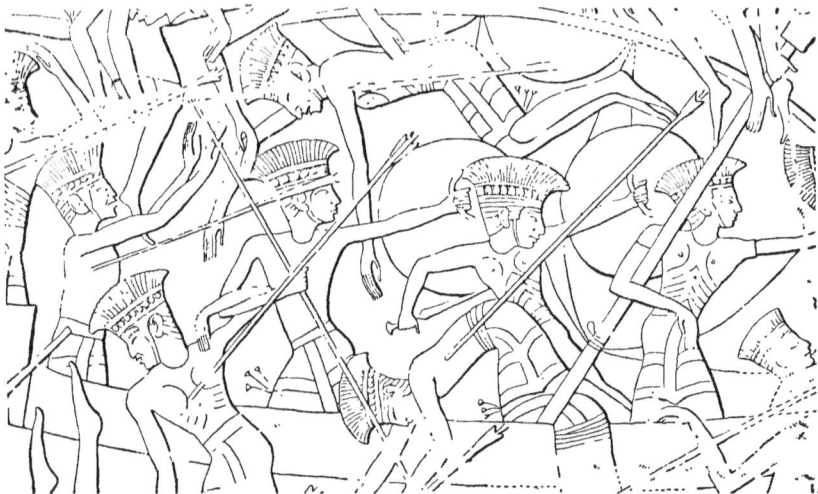

North Sea People in the sea battle. A wounded soldier is falling overboard but is held fast by his comrade. (Medinet Habu).

A large and particularly well-preserved relief shows what happened to the prisoners taken in the battle. They were generally tied together in pairs and taken to the prison camp, where they were forced to sit on the ground, waiting for their interrogation. Then they were led singly before Egyptian officers, distinguishable by their long aprons, and branded with the great name of His Majesty. Afterwards they were taken before an intelligence officer and closely questioned. Their statements under interrogation have been recorded for us by many writers.

The kings and princes of the Northern and sea peoples became the personal captives of the Pharaoh. Ramses III particularly stressed that he had made prisoner the " ten princes " of the Northern peoples and had carried them off in triumph.

The victory of Ramses III seemed complete, but it was in fact only a Pyrrhic victory. He had to give battle several times more, in a lengthy struggle against the North people and the Philistines that is also mentioned in the Bible. The struggle forced Egypt to make heavy sacrifices; in the time of Ramses II she had been still at the height of her power; now she suffered a period of decline and gloomy stagnation. The North people settled in the former Egyptian province of Amor in Syria, colonised the country, and constructed safe harbours along its coast. For nearly two hundred years they ruled Palestine and the Eastern Mediterranean, which came to be known, after the leading tribe of the North people, as the Sea of the Philistines. In alliance with the Libyans they finally succeeded in the invasion of Egypt, when they established a king of military dictatorship. In 946 B.C. a Libyan, Sheshonk I, usurped the Egyptian royal throne.

A comparison of these events, confirmed by contemporary inscriptions and extensive archæological evidence, and the statements of the Atlantis legend, show that all the statements of the legend agree with the historical facts.

We have shown that the legend is correct in recording that, at the beginning of the Iron Age, that is, towards the end of the thirteenth century B.C., during a time of world-wide catastrophes, a powerful people ruling over many islands and countries " near the Great Ocean in the North " united into a single force and set out on a huge military expedition to conquer Greece, Egypt and all the countries of the Mediterranean. This expedition did in fact penetrate through Europe and Asia Minor as far as Egypt, which was seriously threatened; with it were united the Libyans and the Tyrrhenians, the Skekelesh and the Weshesh. The powerful army was in fact commanded by " the Ten," under the supreme command of the King of the Philistines. Strong war chariot units and a powerful navy, which made the only attempt in history to invade Egypt from the sea, reinforced the land army. Great catastrophes occurred during the advance, which was spread over a period of many years. Egypt saved herself from the dire peril that threatened her and preserved her freedom, if only for another hundred or

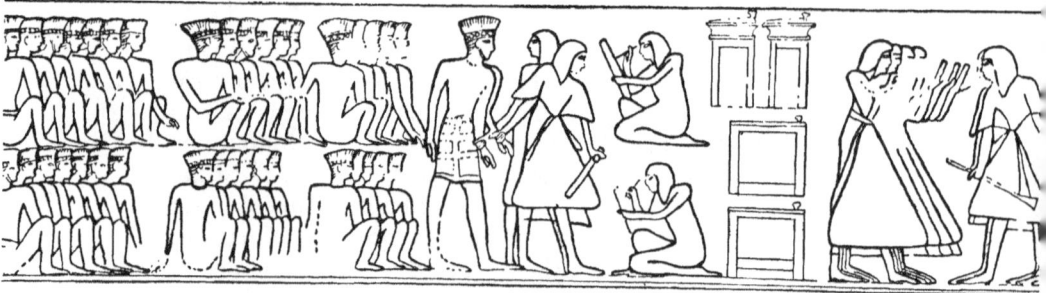

North Sea prisoners waiting to be interrogated.

two hundred years. Ramses III wrote that this great force planned to conquer all the lands of the earth, and in fact it came very near to success; even the captured Northern warriors, after their heavy defeat at his hands, still thought the plan would succeed.

It is simply not possible that Plato, who could not possibly remember these events, or Solon, who admitted that neither he nor any other Greek had even an idea of these happenings, could have invented a description as historically exact as this. The Atlantis legend often corresponds word for word with contemporary original texts, which makes it highly probable that the priests in Sais knew those same inscriptions and papyri, and used them as the basis for their account.

The legend, therefore, must be recognised as an historically valuable, factual report, even though it has hitherto been universally considered as "pure invention." Plato is right when he claims that it is by no means a fairy-tale, but in every respect true history.

### The expedition against Greece: Athens' deliverance

Before the Atlantis people had crossed Asia Minor and Syria and reached the borders of Egypt, they had, according to Plato, succeeded in subjecting all the Greek states. Only Athens preserved her independence and freedom after an heroic struggle. The boundaries of the state of Athens are described in detail, and show that Attica, Oropos and Megara were included within them. The Athenian repulse of the Atlanteans has been described as a shining example of great courage and skilful defence.

Egyptian scribes. The North People are branded with " the Great Name of the King."

This part of the Atlantis legend in particular has been dismissed as unhistorical by scholars. Schulten, who in general upholds the accuracy of the substance of the legend, says that this episode reveals the true reason for Plato's embroidery of the plain facts of the story: he wanted to console himself and the Athenians after the disasters of the Peloponnesian War. Other scholars have said that Plato invented a fairy-tale to glorify his own town of Athens. But even this part of Plato's story is in full accord with the historical facts and archæological finds.

Before the Northern and sea peoples crossed to Asia Minor, they invaded Greece, stormed the fortresses, burned the towns, and brought the Mycenean culture to a speedy and violent end. There is ample evidence of the crushing force with which the North people swept upon Greece.

Historians agree in the great import of this event. Schachermeyer describes it as one of the most terrible catastrophes in the history of the world. According to Wiesner, a storm without parallel swept across the Eastern Mediterranean. Weber believes it to have been nothing less than a world revolution, unparalleled in ancient history in its magnitude and extent. Paret writes that it began a great migration of the peoples of all Central and Southern Europe as well as Asia Minor; it revolutionised the old world and created the basis for the new. Bachofer has called it a flood that determined the destiny of the world.

We cannot, therefore, simply dismiss these events as invented myths or as historical fairy-tales for the comfort of the Athenians. They can be proved to have happened and

4—A

to have created the basis of a new age for the classical, and
therefore for the Western, world.

One astonishing thing is that while Greece, Crete, Asia
Minor and Syria were razed to the ground, Athens and
Attica were left unharmed and unaffected by the collapse
of these peoples. It seems, however, that fighting broke out
between the Athenians and the North people, and that the
fortress slopes of the city were evacuated for a time by the
inhabitants, who sought refuge on the Acropolis. It seems
probable also that the story that King Kodrus, an ancestor
of Solon, was killed in the defence of Athens, contains a germ
of historical truth. It is certain that Athens emerged victorious and preserved her freedom in the way the legend
describes.

In a lecture on the excavations at Cerameicos, the great
cemetery before the gates of Athens, Kubler said that the
immense fortress walls of Athens were only completed in the
late thirteenth century B.C. They were built to protect
the inhabitants, who, as the latest excavations have shown,
evacuated the fortress slopes at this time. The unrest caused
by the Great Migration, which did not finish until the end of
the twelfth century B.C., made itself felt for the first time.
According to finds, languages and tradition, Attica was not
immediately touched by it, but battles did take place, and
we have to assume that some of the pre-Dorian Greek peoples
who were driven from the Peloponnese began a migration
which continued throughout the twelfth century B.C. In this
lies the explanation of the fact that in Athens and Attica
Mycenean pottery continued to be made and developed,
long after the influx of the North people had caused its
disappearance in the rest of Greece.

When we consider that the Northern and sea peoples in
their irresistible advance overwhelmed the rest of Greece,
Crete and the Ægean islands, it is all the more surprising that
in this terrible collapse of the south-eastern lands Athens was
able to preserve her independence.

In conclusion we may say of this episode of Plato's story
that it corresponds without doubt to the historical facts. It is
astonishing, in fact, that Plato did not make more of the

amazing heroic feats of his home town, and that neither Solon nor Plato recognised that these were the battles, reported in Athenian legend, between King Kodrus and the hordes invading from the North. If Plato had been moved to comfort the Athenians, or to praise his ancestors, then without doubt he would have created something different out of the available historical material. He would, for example, have certainly concealed the bitter fact that an enormous number of Athenian warriors were engulfed in the great earthquakes of the period.

How little Plato's account is biased is shown by the one fact that his account, which is supposed to glorify Athens, deals much more extensively with Atlantis. For this reason we have called the story " Legend of Atlantis " and not the " Legend of Ancient Athens."

Plato's intent was clearly not to tell a fable praising the Athenians or glorifying his home town, but to record as faithfully as possible the traditional material.

## 8. CONCLUSIONS

Our inquiry into the questionable part of the Atlantis legend has so far led to the following conclusions:

1. The Atlantis report is in its main aspects a reliable historical source. As Plato repeatedly asserted, it is in fact a Greek adaptation from ancient Egyptian inscriptions and papyri. The events it records did in fact take place in about 1200 B.C. Some of the ancient Egyptian inscriptions and papyri upon which it is based are still in existence, so that we are able to compare their accounts with those of the legend. The comparison shows that Plato and the other traditional sources (the priests of Sais, Solon, Critias the Elder and Critias the Younger) have faithfully reported the accounts given in these texts, and have not been guilty of inventing fables and myths.

If, in spite of this, misunderstandings and errors have crept in, the reason cannot lie in the ancient priests having deliberately falsified the report, but simply in the difficulty of translation and in the fact that somewhere in the long chain of tradition mistakes are bound to occur. The priests made an honest attempt to pass on the records handed down to them to the best of their ability and knowledge; this has been confirmed by Plato. They deserve not bitter complaints and unjust accusations, but thanks and an attentive ear, for they have given us the oldest and most valuable accounts in existence of the history of the Western world, the report of the birth pains and beginnings of Western culture.

Our general attitude towards Plato's report should be one of confident acceptance. Only where clear proofs and undeniable facts speak against certain of Plato's details may we consider an error or misunderstanding in the traditional source. A hasty judgment without investigation is here, as elsewhere, quite unjustified.

2. The second conclusion that we can draw on the basis of our inquiry is that the Atlanteans of the legend are identical with the Northern and sea peoples of the inscriptions and papyri of Ramses III. Our knowledge of these peoples from contemporary texts, backed by that of extensive archæological excavations, is in complete accord with that reported about the Atlanteans. We learn of both that their home was on the islands and lands of the World Ocean in the North; that their land was swept away by storm in an age of terrible drought and great fires; and that their royal town and their country perished at the same time. We learn of both the Atlanteans and the Northern peoples that they combined in a great military expedition, and that the Libyans and the Tyrrhenians were united under them; that they were led by " the Ten " who planned to rule all the lands " to the ends of the earth "; that they conquered Greece, with the exception of Athens, as well as Asia Minor; that they attacked Egypt but their serious threat was successfully repelled. The Atlantis report, like the contemporary reliefs, shows that this great force included powerful chariot groups and a strong navy. There can therefore be no doubt that the term " Atlantis people " is simply another name, probably, a local one, for the Northern and sea peoples.

These two conclusions remove the rubble of misconceptions and the dead weight of unjustified scepticism, hasty dating and misidentifications from the value of the Atlantis legend. They open the way to a treasure chamber of rich historical knowledge and astonishing insight into the life and habits of a great people, living more than three thousand years ago, who were forced to leave their homes in an age of terrible catastrophes.

# SECTION TWO

# THE HOME OF THE ATLANTEANS (NORTH SEA PEOPLES) AND THE LOCATION OF ATLANTIS

## I. THE STATEMENTS OF THE ATLANTIS REPORT AND THE EGYPTIAN TEXTS

AN eminent German philologist once said of those enthusiasts who do not cease in their attempts to solve the question of the homeland of the Atlanteans, that only fools would attempt such a quest. The Austrian art historian R. Noll has described this question as an *idée fixe*. But there are others who do not see why it should be either foolish or an *idée fixe* to try to find the original home of a bygone race which had caused such revolutionary changes in Europe and Asia Minor. After all, this race must have had its home somewhere before being driven to a " Great Migration " through the great natural catastrophes of that age. The Atlantis legend says about the home of the Atlanteans:

1. The Atlanteans came from many islands and part of the mainland by the World Ocean.

2. These islands and coastal strips were situated in the North.

With regard to the first statement, various reports confirm that the many islands and parts of the mainland which were inhabited by the Atlanteans were situated in the World Ocean. Even the repeated statement that Atlantis was situated outside the Pillars of Hercules only underlines the position of that island in the World Ocean. Nowhere in the report does it say that Atlantis was situated to the west, in the vicinity of, or at the Pillars of Hercules, as some Atlantis scholars have erroneously translated. The statement "outside the Pillars" does not give any direction to the locality of Atlantis.

The Egyptians believed that the inhabited earth was shaped like an egg and was encircled by "Oceanos," the Great Water Circle. Ptah, the creator of the universe, is shown on an ancient Egyptian drawing modelling the egg-shape form of the earth. The notion that the Great Water Circle surrounds the inhabited earth is very old and appears already in the fifth dynasty (2650 B.C.), where it is said in a pyramid inscription that the "great round sea," the Great Water Circle, flows around the earth. To the Great Water Circle only the World Seas belong, not the inland seas, like the Mediterreanean. The Mediterranean was called the "Interior Sea." This notion is also predominant in the Atlantis report, where it says that Atlantis was situated beyond the Pillars of Hercules. The ocean in which Atlantis sank did in fact deserve the name "ocean," whilst the sea within the Pillars of Hercules is only a bay with a narrow mouth. It is all too evident that the "exterior"—the World Sea—is not the same as the "Interior Sea," the Mediterranean. The islands of the Atlanteans must therefore be found in the World Sea, and not in the Mediterranean.

With regard to the second statement, the *Dialogues* of Critias specify the direction of Atlantis from Egypt and Greece. It is said that the whole territory was situated "*cataborros*," towards the north. The word "*cataborros*" has often been translated by "protected against the north wind." This is wrong; "*cata*" means "to, in the direction of," "*cata polin*" means "towards the town," "*cat'ouron*" means "in the air," etc., but not "protected against the town," or "against the air." "*Cataborros*" clearly means "towards the north wind," and not "protected against the north wind."

We must therefore place Atlantis to the north of Egypt and Greece in the World Ocean, as is said in the Atlantis report. Contemporary texts completely agree with this location. We read in them about the North people that they came from the Great Water Circle from the end of the earth, and that their island homeland was situated in the North. These people have therefore rightly been called the " sea people," or North people, or " peoples from the Islands of the Seas." Other sources concerning the home of these people confirm these statements. In the inscriptions of Medinet Habu and in the Papyrus Harris it is said that the North people came from the end of the earth, or from the " great darkness." The first statement, that the North people came from the ends of the earth, is also confirmed in Old Testament and traditional Greek sources. The Philistines, the leading tribe of the North people, are described as descendants of Japhet, who undoubtedly is identical with the Japetos of Greek mythology. Homer has related that Japetos' home was at the farthest end of the earth and Oceanos. And in the Old Testament, the people of Israel, who were invading Palestine, were threatened in the case of disobedience against God with the " people at the end of the earth," a clear allusion to the forthcoming serious battles with the Philistines. According to Greek tradition Atlas, the first king of the Atlanteans, was the eldest son of Japetos. Atlas also rules " at the ends of the earth."

According to contemporary inscriptions and traditional fables the home of the Northern and sea peoples is therefore situated " at the ends of the earth." By this expression was meant the farthest North, and not the West, as was believed later. With the Egyptians, the description " ends of the earth " was an established mode of speech for the lands in the far North. They also used the expression " the northern countries at the end of the earth." Behind the description of the far North lies the ancient notion, later replaced by the notion of the global earth, that the earth was shaped like a cow, standing with its horns towards the south and with its tail towards the north. For this reason the early Egyptians described the farthest south as the " earth's horns," and the farthest north as " the earth's tail." This notion of the earth cow, which is fertilised by the " heavenly bull," has in all probability been taken over by the Indo-Germanic peoples. Strangely, even Kepler has utilised the picture of the earth cow.

When in ancient writings the expression " ends of the earth " is used we have to think primarily in terms of the " farthest North." Only in later times, as late perhaps as the fourth century B.C., may other directions be meant by this expression.

Other expressions for the farthest North include: Borders of darkness, united darkness, homes of the night, sources of the night, farthest—or deepest—darkness. The notion that the land of darkness is situated in the far North could be attributed to knowledge of the long Nordic winter nights. Statements in the *Amduat*, the Book of the Darkness, show quite clearly that the Egyptians looked for the darkness, " the united darkness," in the North only, and not in any other direction. We can, therefore, interpret the statement that the North people " come out of the darkness " or " escape into the darkness " as meaning that their origin was in the far North.

The phrase " at the columns of heaven " is also descriptive of the farthest North. As the Pole Star appears to be the only fixed point in the sky, the idea arose very early in man's history that in the far North stood columns upon which the sky rested. For example, the Egyptians believed that " the gods carrying the sky lived in the farthest North." Similarly, the Greeks meant the farthest North when they said that Atlas, the son of Japetos, standing before the dwellings of the night, carried the far sky on bowed head and untiring hands at the ends of the earth.

The Atlantis report reveals in detail that the Atlanteans not only knew of this belief in the column supporting the sky, but actually believed that the column stood in the centre of their temple. The Old Testament confirms that they cherished this belief even after their migration from the north to the Mediterranean lands. The name given to them in the Old Testament is " Caphtorites "—column people, and their home island was " ai Caphtor "—column island. There are drawings of sky columns on ceramics, and for astronomical reasons O. S. Reuter firmly believed that the home of the sky column cult was in the North.

When therefore Ramses III speaks of his victory over the

peoples " of the borders of united darkness, the ends of the earth and the columns of heavens," he is undoubtedly emphasising that these peoples originally came from the far north.

## 2. THE THEORIES PUT FORWARD UP TO THE PRESENT ABOUT THE HOMELAND OF THE NORTH SEA PEOPLES

The Yugoslav historian Milojcic, in his book on the archæological remains of the North people who invaded Greece in 1200 B.C., says that undoubtedly the most difficult problem is to ascertain the starting-point of the great migration. Eissfeld says that the burning question of the origin of the North peoples is as unsettled today as it was two thousand years ago. Other scholars have also called it a puzzling and hitherto unsolved problem.

The following ideas have been put forward about the homeland of the North Sea people, or Philistines, the leading tribe of the North Sea people's coalition:

The German Egyptologist Bilabel seeks the homeland of the North Sea people in the neighbourhood of Sinai, or in Southern Syria. Schachermeyr thinks that only the culture-less lands of Europe and secondly the barbaric parts of Asia Minor can be considered as the homelands of the migrating people. Petrie thinks that these people might have originated from Crete, because one of the North Sea people is called Sakar, or Zakar, in the Egyptian inscriptions, and there is a place called Zakro, at the east coast of Crete from whence this people might have come. The archæologist Fimmen thought that all these people must originate from the islands and coasts of the Ægean Sea. But these attempts at identi-fication with known national tribes are as numerous as they are diverse, and we cannot be certain of any of them. The German historian Wiesner believes that the point of departure of the Philistine migration was situated in the Danubian-Balkan territory. Milojcic assumes the homeland of these peoples to be in the north-eastern part of present-day Yugoslavia. Friedrich Wirth says that these tribes must have once lived to the north of the great Danube territory.

Schuchhardt, the great prehistoric scholar, believes their homeland to be in Middle and Northern Germany, Herbig in Silesia and Eastern Germany, Kayser, the director of the Egyptian Museum in Hildesheim, in Italy or Spain.

But all these beliefs conflict with the contemporary Egyptian inscriptions, the extensive archæological material and the course of the migration.

In principal the following territories have to be excluded when searching for the homeland of the North Sea people:

1. Those territories destroyed or conquered by them. No people destroys its own homeland.

2. The territories situated inland, far from the sea. " Sea people," or " people from the Islands of the Sea," whose islands have been swept away by storms, cannot come from inland.

3. Territories situated in any direction other than north of Egypt. In the Egyptian inscriptions the origin of the peoples " from the North " would not have been stressed so frequently had they originated from another direction.

4. Territories which cannot be included for archæological reasons. Many remains of these peoples have been found in parts they destroyed or occupied, and we cannot search for their homeland in parts where their remains are foreign and unknown.

For these reasons it is basically wrong to look for the homeland of the North Sea people around Sinai, in Palestine, in Asia Minor, on the Ægean Islands, in Crete, Greece or Macedonia. Numerous excavations in these parts have given ample proof that they had been destroyed by the invading North people around 1200 B.C. Milojcic has therefore stressed the point that the conquering people must have had their home north of the line Macedonia–Thracia–Hellespont.

In the countries north of this line, which have been suggested as the home of the North Sea people—North-Eastern Yugoslavia, Hungary, Central and Southern Germany, Silesia and Eastern Germany—there are no islands or World Ocean, and it is improbable that people skilled in sea navigation, like the North people, could have come from these parts.

Italy and Spain can also not be considered as the home of the North people, because migrating tribes aiming for Egypt would not have chosen to move across Macedonia, Asia Minor and Syria, but would have crossed directly to North Africa to unite there with the Libyans for an attack against Egypt. It is, furthermore, certain that the archæological material left behind by the North people in their migration did not originate from Italy or Spain. Also Italy is not situated at the " World Ocean "; Spain is not north, but west of Egypt.

All hitherto established theories concerning the homelands of the North Sea people are therefore in contradiction to the above-mentioned methodical principles and must be rejected. Only the territories which in prehistory are called the " Nordic parts," comprising Northern Hanover, Schleswig-Holstein, Denmark and Sweden, with Oland and Gotland, can be reckoned to have been the departing points of these peoples.

### 3. ARCHÆOLOGICAL EVIDENCE FOR THE ORIGIN OF THE NORTH SEA PEOPLES IN THE NORTH SEA AREA

When contemporary Egyptian inscriptions and the Atlantis report both agree that the North Sea people, or Atlanteans, originated in the islands and coasts of the " World Ocean " in the North, we have to ascertain whether we can confirm or deny these statements on the basis of the archæological remains of these people.

In the layers of ruins in the Eastern Mediterranean we frequently find remains which we have to ascribe to these people. In some regions the Norse peoples introduced forms and methods which were unknown before their arrival. The Egyptian reliefs give us the necessary information about the characteristics of the North Sea people. This extensive material will now be investigated to determine whether it originated from the area of the present North Sea.

As early as 1870 the archæologist A. Konze ascertained in a detailed study of the ceramics which appeared after the destruction of the Mycenic culture in the South-Eastern parts that there is an undeniable relationship between these ceramics and those of the North-Eastern European peoples. This view has often been repeated and never been denied.

These ceramics, called "sub-Mycenic" and "proto-geometric," show a certain advance on that of the Nordic area, and sometimes betray a similarity to the vanished Mycenic art, because some of the Achæic potters continued to work for their new masters. Friedrich Wirth collected the archæological material in 1938 and declared that the Nordic origin of the North Sea people is thereby firmly established. We can confirm Wirth's assertion by a short survey.

In the layers of ruins, or the caves which were laid out in 1200 B.C., we repeatedly find from Greece to Egypt tang-swords, flame-like spear-tops and umbos of shields, those weapons which are also shown on the contemporary reliefs of the North Sea people. Wiesner calls these weapons characteristic new forms of the Great Migration.

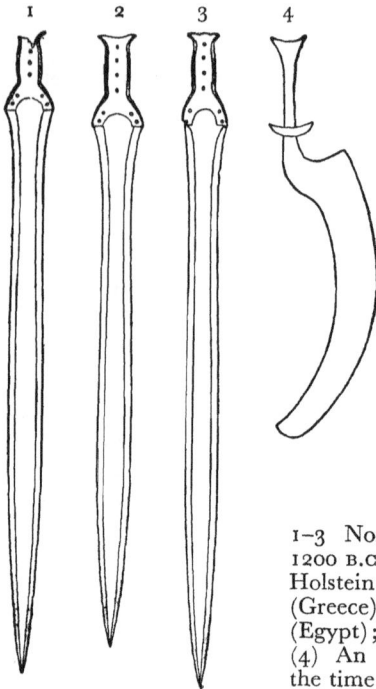

1–3 Northern tang-swords of 1200 B.C.: (1) From Schleswig-Holstein; (2) From Mycene (Greece); (3) From Bubatsis (Egypt);
(4) An Egyptian sword from the time of 1200 B.C.

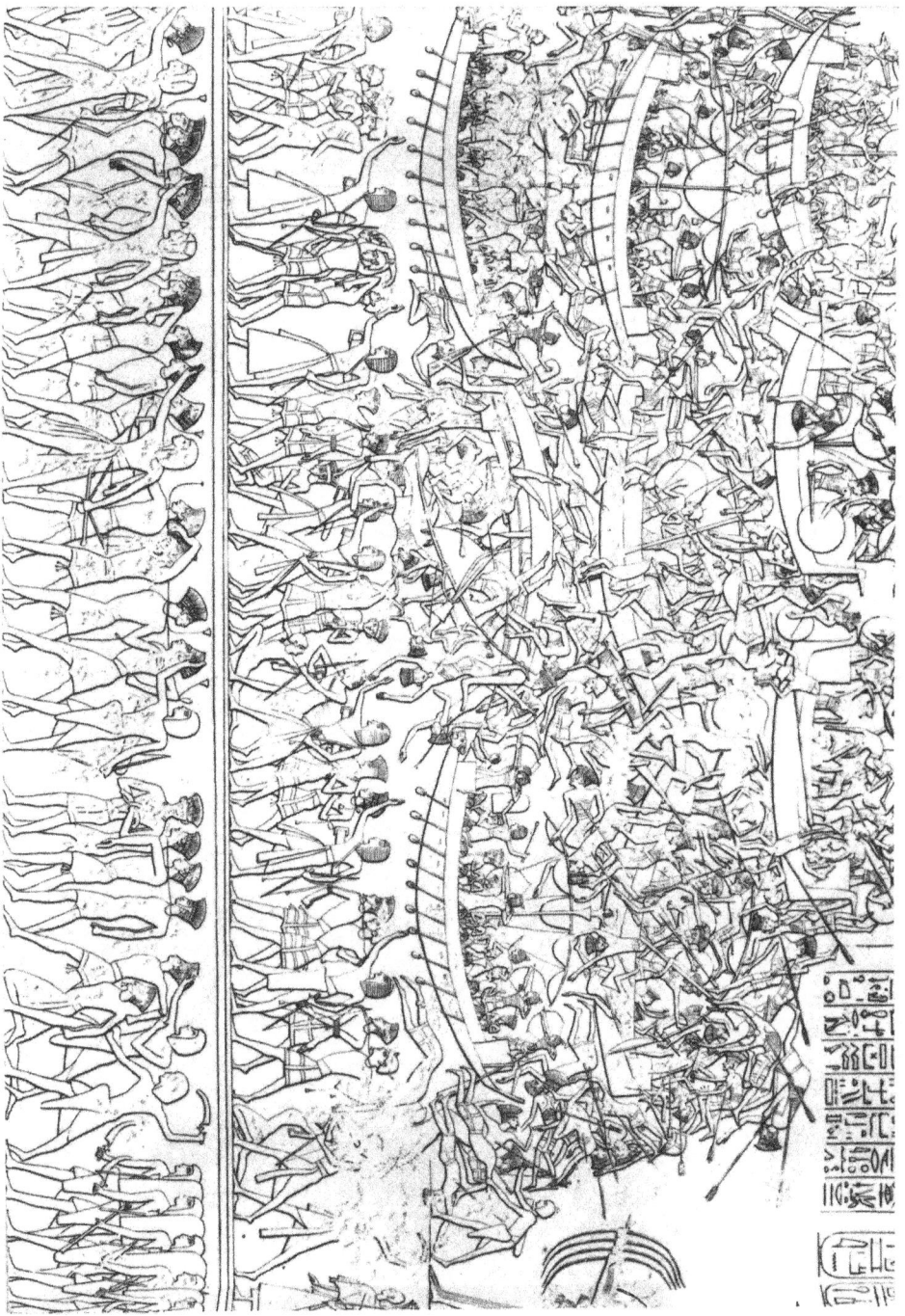

The sea battle between the North Sea People and the Egyptians, 1195 B.C.

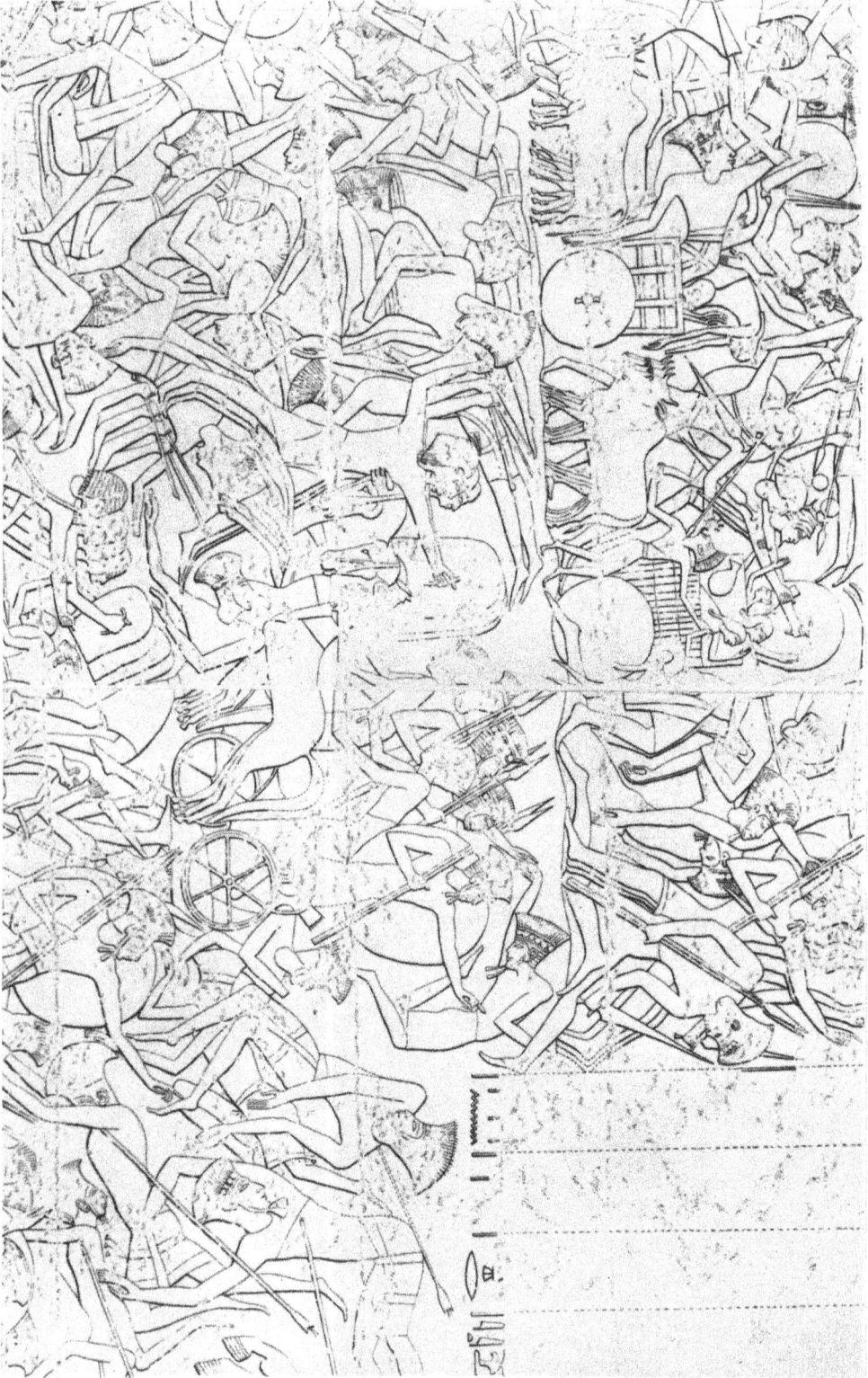

Section from the Relief depicting the land battle between the North Sea People and the Egyptians, 1195 B.C.

Kossina, the German scholar on prehistory, says of these tang-swords that they could as well have been found in Pomerania and Holstein (Northern Germany). Behn is of the opinion that the bronze tang-swords of a Nordic shape which were found in Egypt were carried by Germanic mercenaries in the Egyptian forces.

As these weapons are first found in the layers of ruins dated around 1200 B.C., and as at that time no Germanic mercenaries fought on the side of the Egyptians, they could only have been brought into the South-Eastern area by hordes of Nordic soldiers and not by merchants or mercenaries.

The tang-sword is found in vast quantities in Nordic parts in the thirteenth century B.C., a fact which has been confirmed by Sprockhoff, the greatest expert on these swords. According to him the extensive use of the Germanic tang-sword is a proof of the extent of the area of Germanic colonisation. The flame-like spear-tops which were frequently found in the layer of ruins around 1200 B.C. in the South-Eastern area appear also in the fourth period in the Nordic area in vast quantities. Amongst them have been discovered specimens which, like the tang-swords, have their exact counterparts in the Nordic area and almost appear to originate from the same armourer's workshop. Here also it is important for chronological reasons to know that flame-like spear-tops were very frequent in the Nordic area in Periods I and II, were absent in Period III and reappeared in their old forms in Period IV.

The round shield also, as carried by the North Sea peoples during their invasion of the South-Eastern area, appears in the Nordic area very early. We know, for example, the presentation of men with spears and round shields on the Horn of Wismar, which Norden, the Swedish expert on prehistory, ascribed on the basis of its ornamentation to the later part of Period II. Numerous drawings of warriors with round shields are to be found on Scandinavian rock reliefs, whilst some bronze round shields from the Nordic area are also known in their original state.

In Greece, during the time of Mycenes, there existed the great, double-tailed shield, which like armour-plating

5—A

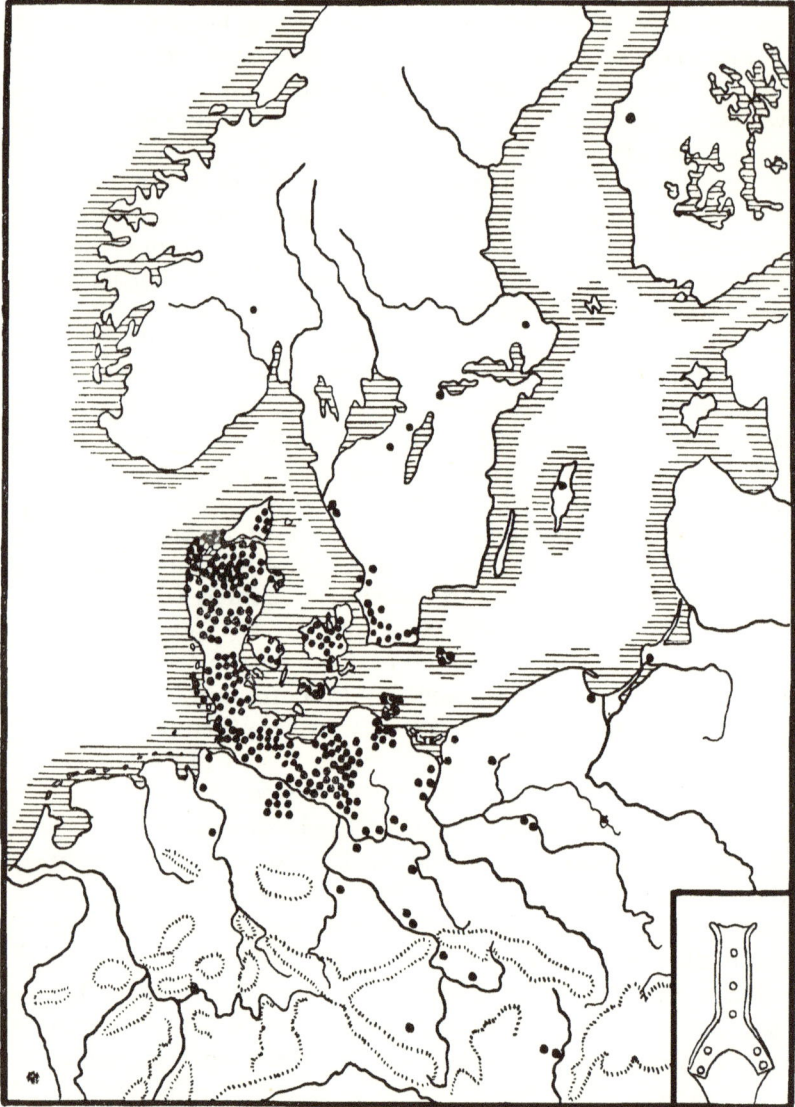

Distribution of the ordinary German tang-sword of 1200 B.C.

protected the whole body, whilst in Egypt contemporary reliefs show that a long, arched shield was carried.

Apart from the weapons, the ships which were built by the North Sea people for their attack against Egypt are a further proof of the origin of these peoples in the North Sea area.

These ships, known to us from the reliefs in Medinet Habu, had not been seen in the Mediterranean before; they differ basically from all other types of ships used until then in this area. The ships of the North Sea people have at their bow and stern a steeply rising stem decorated by a swan or dragon head. The rudder control was aft the quarter-deck; the sails, in contrast to the method then used in the Mediterranean, were set without lower sails, and could be secured without the help of special knots. It was therefore possible to set the sails quickly from the deck. The protective covering of the ship was raised considerably at the bow and stern; a high board prevented rough seas from swamping the ship and protected at the same time the crew sitting behind. The mast could be laid down, and carried on top a basket-like construction. All these constructional characteristics had until then not existed in the Mediterranean and were taken over by the Egyptians from the North people.

Similar types of ships exist during the Bronze Age only on Nordic rock drawings. The Brandskogenship, for example, is a type of ship which is remarkably like those of the North people, apart from the sails, which are not shown. Herbig says of the ships of the North Sea people on the Egyptian reliefs that they at first remind one of Nordic ships and of the much later Viking dragon ships. He says that these ships are foreign to the Eastern Mediterranean and had been brought in from elsewhere.

Anyone with some knowledge of navigational matters can see at once, when looking at the ships of the North people, that their builders were experienced shipwrights. They had constructed in these ships splendid high-sea craft which can be regarded as wellnigh perfect and have been the prototype of sailing ships until the present day. These ships and the historical fact of an attack across the Mediterranean are

Northern round shields
(Bronze).

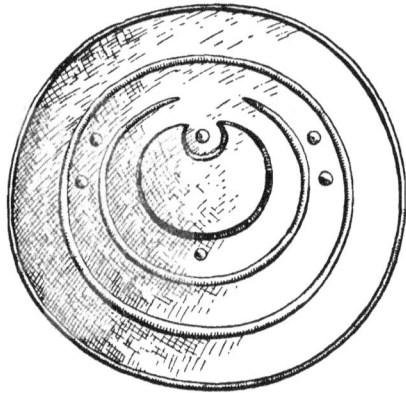

Rock drawing from Bohuslän
(Sweden).

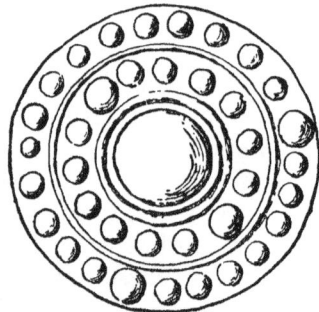

Northern round shield from
Wittenham.

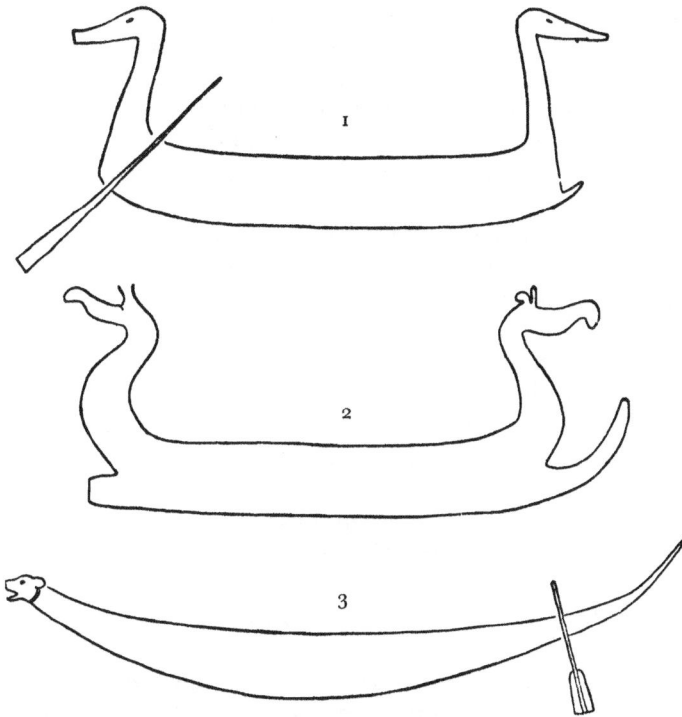

Ships from the period of 1200 B.C.: (1) Ship of the North Sea Peoples (Medinet Habu); (2) Brandskogen ship (Swedish rock drawing); (3) Egyptian warship (Medinet Habu).

proof that the North Sea people were the most experienced sailors of their times.

Apart from the weapons and ships the costumes of the North Sea people had until then been unknown in the Mediterranean. The only parallel to such costumes is to be found in the Nordic area. In the wall pictures of Medinet Habu the North people wear either the so-called rush-blade crown or the horn helm. The rush-blade crown is held by Herbig to be an " Illyrian characteristic," whilst the Philistines, the leading tribe of the North people coalition, were considered by him to be Illyrians.

But the Philistines were not Illyrians; of them in particular the contemporary inscriptions say that they came " from the islands." In the Illyrian area (Silesia and Eastern Germany) there were no islands. Furthermore, during the period in question, archæological material reveals no Illyrians in either Greece or Asia Minor. This kind of head decoration has not been found in the Illyrian area, but the Nordic rock pictures of the Bronze Age show this decoration on male figures. It is possible that the so-called " ray crowns " worn by some male figures can be described as rush-blade crowns.

The horn helmets worn by some of the North people were also unknown in the Mediterranean, but they are repeatedly presented on Bronze Age rock pictures in the Nordic area. Some examples have been found in the North Sea area.

The clothing shown on the North people in the reliefs corresponds with the clothing which was used during the Bronze Age in the Nordic area. The chief garment of the men was, according to contemporary Egyptian reliefs, a knee-length apron, held by a belt decorated by a tuft around the hips and worn with a shoulder piece. Men's aprons similar to these were frequently found in the Nordic graves of the Bronze Age.

Some of the men's figures on the reliefs also wear a coat made from one piece which reaches as far as the ankle. These coats are also known solely in the Nordic area and have been preserved in oak coffins on Jutland dating from the fourteenth and fifteenth centuries B.C. Schwantes calls these Nordic coats a singularly beautiful creation, a technical masterpiece, obviously the result of a long weaving tradition. According to Schuchhardt these coats came to Greece through the Great Migration and were later widely used under the name of " chlamys."

Besides clothing the hair style of the North Sea people is a sign of their origin. On Egyptian reliefs some captured Norse warriors wear a side plait at the temple. According to Alian, the kings of Atlantis wore a side plait as a sign of divinity. Although we do not know a Bronze Age skull with such a side plait, numerous hair combs found in Nordic graves of this epoch show that the men wore their hair long and possibly with a side plait.

On a moor in Schleswig-Holstein a man's skull was found in 1947 originating from the third or fourth century on which a side plait could be seen.

Tacitus reports that the Swabians, who lived at that time in the Nordic area, tied their hair over the ear in a knot; this was called by the Romans " *nodus suebicus*," or Swabian knot. Many Germanic pictures of the Iron Age show this side plait. Behn thinks that without doubt this custom goes back to much more ancient times. The male members of the Merowing royal household wore the side plait as a sign of royal rank as late as the Middle Ages.

All warriors of the North Sea people are shown on the Egyptian wall pictures as clean shaven. The Mycenic gold masks show that Greek men in the Mycenic period wore a full beard. In the Nordic area razors have been found in graves as early as Period II; these finds are more frequent in the third and fourth periods and confirm the pictures on the Egyptian reliefs.

New funeral and burial customs reached the Eastern Mediterranean through the Great Migration. In Asia Minor, on the Ægean islands, on Crete especially and, less frequently, on the Greek mainland, corpse burning was prevalent. This procedure is the more remarkable since in the time of 1200 B.C. in the whole area of Aegea, Syria, Mesopotamia and Asia Minor only the burial rites were customary. The great mound, which then appeared in the Eastern Mediterranean, was unknown there before 1200 B.C. In the Nordic area, however, it appeared in many earlier periods. Corpse burning was widespread at the time of migration from the Nordic area, during the fourth period.

Schuchhardt has pointed out that an earth wall construction which was quite unknown in the south came to Greece with the Great Migration. Earth walls were erected for the protection of camps and towns, and were equipped in front with stakes. These earth walls existed only in prehistoric Germany. We shall hear that the royal town of Atlantis was protected by this " Nordic dike construction." The Dutch scholar Van Griffen has been able to shown in his excavation of Bronze Age mounds that this construction existed from the existence of stake holes, or the remains of stakes still visible nowadays.

It may be also worth mentioning that a peculiar kind of riding appeared with the Great Migration. A lightly armed soldier and a rider both sat on the horse, the soldier jumping off at the beginning of the battle. The Greeks called this new style of riding " *amipos.*" According to the Atlantis report, this custom was also prevalent amongst the Atlanteans and was later confirmed by the Teutons.

It is certain that the North people brought iron with them into the South-East. We shall devote a chapter to this problem later, but may point out now that neither in Greece, the Balkan peninsula, Hungary nor Central Germany was the technique of iron production known until then. It is impossible for the North people to have acquired the metallurgy of iron or the skill and necessary experience for working iron to make arms and tools during the Migration. At least some of the North Sea people must have known iron technique before they started on their great journey. In fact iron tools were found in the Nordic area in the thirteenth and fourteenth centuries B.C. The North Sea people therefore did not acquire the knowledge of iron in Asia Minor, but brought it with them from their Nordic homes. In the Atlantis report it is stated that the Atlanteans knew of iron, and this is confirmed without doubt by historical facts.

The way the North Sea people are presented on Egyptian reliefs underlines the fact that the Atlanteans came from the North. Herbig says that the Egyptian artists have drawn the Philistines as people of pure Nordic type, tall and slender figures, with long skulls, straight nose and high forehead. Schachermeyr says about these drawings that they represent European, even Nordic types.

Everything, therefore, from the representations on the Egyptian reliefs to the archæological finds of that period, points to the fact that these people did in fact originate from the North Sea area.

4.  ARCHÆOLOGICAL EVIDENCE FOR THE MIGRATION OF THE
    NORTH SEA PEOPLES FROM THE NORDIC AREA

The question now arises whether a migration of considerable sections of people from the Nordic area at the end of the
twelfth century B.C. can either be proved or, at least, made to
appear probable.

Before we raise this question we must point out that the
establishment of migrations from archæological arguments
is by no means as easy as is often assumed. Wolff confirms this
when he says that it is significant that in later periods, known
to us through historical sources, such occurrences can hardly
be proved in the literal sense of the term. Whilst, therefore,
proofs of historically known migrations in the later periods
cannot be borne out by archæological means, we may regard
it as evidence that this migration from the Nordic area at the
end of the thirteenth century B.C. was extensive and of the
greatest consequence.

We have already established in earlier chapters that the
North Sea people, on their way through Europe and Asia
Minor to Egypt, left behind them weapons of the Nordic
Bronze Age, whilst weapons of Period III were completely
absent. Other equipment of Period III was also absent, for
example the Nordic battle-axe, which also disappeared in
the North in Period IV. It follows from this that the Great
Migration began in the North shortly before 1200 B.C.
during Period IV. We have therefore to fix the beginning
Period IV fifty or one hundred years later.*

---

\* Kossina divides the Bronze Age into five periods and dates these as follows:

|           |     |     |     |     | B.C.      |
|-----------|-----|-----|-----|-----|-----------|
| Period I  | ... | ... | ... | ... | 2300–1750 |
| Period II, a, b, c | ... | ... | ... | ... | 1750–1400 |
| Period III, a, b | ... | ... | ... | ... | 1400–1150 |
| Period IV | ... | ... | ... | ... | 1150–1000 |
| Period V  | ... | ... | ... | ... | 1000– 750 |

Montelius divides the Bronze Age into six periods with the following dates

|           |     |     |     |     | B.C.      |
|-----------|-----|-----|-----|-----|-----------|
| Period I  | ... | ... | ... | ... | 1800–1500 |
| Period II | ... | ... | ... | ... | 1500–1300 |
| Period III | ... | ... | ... | ... | 1300–1100 |
| Period IV | ... | ... | ... | ... | 1100–1000 |
| Period V  | ... | ... | ... | ... | 1000– 750 |
| Period VI | ... | ... | ... | ... | 750– 600 |

The discovery of a tang-sword, upon which the name Sethos II was engraved, was decisive for the dating so far. This sword is completely similar to those of the Nordic area. Unfortunately, the hilt of this sword was destroyed—the main characteristics which enable a sword to be dated in a particular period are found on the hilt—and we cannot therefore decide whether it belongs to Period III or IV. We have, however, to arrive somehow at a dating of the Germanic Bronze Age periods: it was therefore assumed that this tang-sword belonged to Period III. It came to Egypt in the middle of its style period and a style period lasted about two hundred years. A number of uncertain factors therefore form the basis for the dating of Period III, which is given as between 1300 and 1150 B.C.

We possess much more reliable proofs for the dating of the transition from Period III to Period IV. When, in the cycle of destruction around 1200 B.C., typical articles of Period IV of the Nordic Bronze Age appear in Greece and Egypt, but articles of Period III are absent, then Period IV must have begun in the Nordic area shortly before 1200 B.C.

We shall fix Period IV as starting in the last decades of the thirteenth century B.C. We are supported by the following observations: contemporary Egyptian inscriptions, the Atlantis report and archæological finds prove that the invasion of the North people into the South-East area must have been a unified undertaking by an organised state machine. This view is supported by the wall pictures in Medinet Habu. All North people carried the same sword, most of them two spears and a round shield, and all wore the same kind of apron and helmet. It is obvious that an army with uniform clothing and weapons marched against Egypt. We may conclude from this that the North people were already uniformly clothed and armed for their expedition in their homeland. The embellished and ostentatious arms of Period III have disappeared, and in their place are arms, shields and helmets which were less decorative but more effective in battle. Even in those days plans of world conquest, as shown on contemporary Egyptian reliefs, required an enormous rearmament programme and a unified and organised army. We can conclude that the change of weapons from Period III to Period IV took place in the Nordic area towards the end of the thirteenth century B.C. The migration must therefore have taken place during Period IV of the Nordic Bronze Age.

It can in fact be proved archæologically that a great migration from the Nordic area started at the beginning of Period IV. The German scholar H. Hoffmann has proved in his work on the later Bronze Age that since Period IV an enormous quantity of deposit finds were discovered in the Nordic area. Deposit finds are, according to Hoffmann, a significant proof of migratory movements, a view shared by many other scholars. O. Paret is also of the opinion that the enormous number of deposits which had been left behind from the North Sea to the Mediterranean clearly show the flight route of the North people. He says that during the climatic catastrophes the motto must have been: Save yourselves at all cost! Many must have taken their metal possessions with them, but left these *en route* in order to make their escape easier. The extent of the treasure finds can therefore be recognised as flight routes rather than routes of commerce.

According to Hoffmann we can draw the following conclusions from the deposit finds in the Nordic area:

1. The migration, or flight, began at first in the North.

2. The whole Nordic area was affected by the great migratory movement during Period IV.

3. The migration took place from north to south. Whilst in the North the grave finds decreased strongly, the deposit finds increased steadily at the same time.

4. In the Nordic area the grave finds (settlements) and deposit finds (flight routes) are not found together.

Hoffmann explains this fact with the remark that the flight routes avoided the settlements in order to avoid conflicts.

As the North people in no way avoided conflicts during their migration, but usually attacked with tremendous fury, and as the cautious avoidance of settled parts can only be ascertained north of the River Elbe, we must assume that the Northern tribes were in alliance with those settlements. This fact is also underlined by contemporary Egyptian inscriptions and the Atlantis report.

On their way south the North people went along the Rivers Elbe and Danube. They drove the Illyrians from their homes on the upper reaches of the River Elbe. Some of the Illyrians were probably carried off by the Northmen, but there is no archæological proof that the Illyrians existed at that time in the South-East. The greater part of the Illyrians fled to the Eastern Alps and from there to Apulia and Venetia.

It has often been assumed that the Illyrians were the original cause of the Great Migration, and took a considerable part in the occupation of Greece and the destruction of Mycenæan culture. But the Illyrians themselves were in distress and involved in the conflict. At that period they appeared in the South-East and entered Greece only two to three hundred years later.

The North Sea people advanced towards the end of the thirteenth century across Silesia, Bohemia and Moravia into the Hungarian Plain and there is a possibility that they stayed there for a time, leaving behind a large part of their people. In the Hungarian area there are a great number of deposit finds of weapons and articles similar to those often found in the Northern territories.

From Hungary the North Sea people moved down the Danube; some went to Asia Minor via the Bosphorus, others through Greece and the Pelopennese to Crete. All along the route of the Northmen were found numerous deposits and burial installations, in which the main weapons of the fourth period of the Nordic Bronze Age were left behind.

In conclusion we can establish without doubt that a migration of large groups of people from the Nordic area to the south in Period IV can be proved by prehistorical research. The enormous amount of deposit finds and the numerous finds of Nordic origin along the Rivers Elbe and Danube, and in Hungary, Greece, Crete, Asia Minor, Syria and Egypt show clearly that the statement of the Atlantis report, that the Atlanteans or North Sea people crossed Europe and Asia Minor into Egypt, corresponds with historical fact.

### 5. THE NAMES OF THE RACES

In contemporary Egyptian inscriptions the names of several races of the North Sea people's coalition have been preserved. The Egyptians distinguish between three tribes, or races, amongst the North Sea people: the Phrst, the Sakar and the Denes, names that help us to identify these races later with races inhabiting the Eastern Mediterranean

In the first place are named the " Phrst," pronounced " Pelest," " Pherest," " Pulasati " and Philistines, as the pronunciation of Egyptian letters is uncertain. The Philistines played a leading rôle during the attack on Egypt, and also during the subsequent period.

All scholars who occupy themselves with the happenings of that age are in complete agreement that the " Phrst " of the Egyptian inscriptions are identical with the Philistines of the Old Testament. We shall therefore also call this leading race of the North Sea people Philistines, without deciding whether the Semitic pronunciation of the name of that North people is correct.

The Philistines come " from the islands," a statement confirmed by the Old Testament, where it says: " The Philistines which are left of the island Caphtor " (Jeremiah xlvii. 4). Egyptian sources also state that the islands of the Philistines in the north were " torn out and swept away by the wind." According to Schachermeyr the Philistines erected on Crete a great sea kingdom, which included as its main support the Palestinian coast. Soon they ruled over the whole of the Eastern Mediterranean to such an extent that the Mediterranean received the name " Sea of the Philistines."

Along the flat, sandy coast of Palestine, with few harbours and treacherous to shipping, the Philistines built splendid natural harbours. The towns of Gaza, Askalon, Asdod, Jamnia, Dor, Achsip and Byblos flourished and united to form a league of free towns which has been compared by the American archæologist E. Grant with the Hansa league of the North German towns during the Middle Ages.

Askalon, the " Bride of Syria," soon overtook all other towns. A king of the Philistines resided there and was also called " King of the Askalons." The name " Askalon " is unknown in Semitic languages and is probably a Philistine and Nordic name.

The Philistines gained fame through the fact that they were the first iron experts to enter the South-East area. The oldest iron implements are found in their graves, and the oldest iron furnaces were found in the land of the Philistines. We know from the Old Testament that the Philistines exercised a kind of monopoly in the production of iron, and even knew how to make steel, which, however, they kept secret.

Their battles with the people of Israel have been described in detail in the writings of the Old Testament. The continual threat of the Philistines was the actual cause of the creation of the kingdom and state of Israel.

Closely connected with the Philistines are the " Sakar," a name written by the Egyptologist Grapow " Zeker," by the well-known historian E. Meyer " Zakari," and by Schachermeyr " Takara."

The Sakar took part in the attack against Egypt with the Philistines by land as well as by sea. Like the Philistines they were skilled navigators and in their weapons and clothing are difficult to distinguish from them.

By a stroke of good fortune a papyrus from the time around 1095 B.C. has been preserved for us. Its title reads: " Concerning the journey of officials from the temple of Amons, Wen-Amun, to procure wood for the great, wonderful barge of Amon-Re, King of the Gods." We learn from this papyrus that the Sakar had a king in those days in Dor with the name of Bender who ruled over the surrounding coastal parts. The behaviour of this Sakar prince towards the Egyptian temple official, who was in distress because one of his sailors had made off with the ship's purse, betrays strong legal consciousness and a noble human attitude. We also learn from this papyrus that the Sakar possessed a strong navy, and it is reported that eleven Sakar ships left the harbour of Byblos at the same time. As this papyrus has only been preserved by good fortune we must assume that the Sakar had other settlements in the Eastern Mediterranean.

The Sakar are not mentioned in the writings of the Old Testament, as evidently the Israelites could not distinguish between the Philistines and Sakar, and thought both races to be the same.

Petrie believes that, on account of the similarity between the name of Sakar and the place Zakro, on the east coast of Crete, the Sakro originated from Zakro. But this assumption is rejected by Schachermeyr, who questions the method on which it is based.

For the same reason we have to reject the idea that the Sakar are identical with the Teukrers. According to Greek sources the Teukrers lived in Troad in Asia Minor. Their country had also been destroyed by the Northmen around 1200 B.C. The Teukrers lived in the Troad before 1200 B.C., whilst the Sakar and other North tribes did not reach that part until their migration around 1200 B.C. and did not settle there. Contemporary Egyptian inscriptions prove that the Sakar, like the Philistines, originate from the North countries near the World Sea, or North Sea.

The Egyptian inscriptions mention a third tribe, the " Denes," a word pronounced by E. Meyer " Danuna " and by Schachermeyr " Denjen." This tribe is also always linked with the Philistines, and its people are particularly called " Denes from the islands." Here again faulty method has been employed to identify the Denes with the Danai. According to Greek tradition the Danai had their homes in the Argolis, which was completely laid bare by the North Sea people. Schachermeyr recognises the difficulty of identification and proposes as the only solution the assumption that the Danai were probably forced into service by the barbarians, who were not used to navigation, and they became enemies of the Egyptians against their will. But this assumption is invalid from every point of view. The Philistines and the other North Sea people were not unskilled in navigational matters; they were the most experienced sailors of their age. These people were not obliged to force other tribes into sea service, but knew how to build ships superior to those of the Achæans in every way, and they themselves steered the dragon ships across the sea. The Egyptian wall pictures do not reveal any pressed Achæans on the ships of the Northmen. All crews on these ships carry the same arms, clothing and the same head decorations as the Northmen of the land forces. Furthermore it must be noted that the Danai were already settled in the Argolis by 1400 B.C., whilst the Denes, together with other Northmen, did not invade that country until 1200 B.C.

There is no doubt that the Denes belong to the Philistines and the Sakar, and, like them, originate from the North Sea area, the royal kingdom of Atlantis.

The Sekelese, Sardana and Vasasa, who are mentioned by the Egyptian inscriptions as allies of the Northmen, play a subordinate rôle and do not belong to the Northmen proper. They appear much earlier as mercenaries in Egypt and fight during the battles of the North Sea people on the side of Ramses III. In all probability the Sardana are identical with the inhabitants of Sardinia, the Sekelese with the inhabitants of Sicily, and the Vasasa with the inhabitants of other islands in the Mediterranean, perhaps the Balearic.

The fact that these tribes partly fought on the side of the Northmen, and partly on the side of the Egyptians, is a confirmation of the statements in the Atlantis report that the Atlanteans subjected the territories of the Tyrrhenian Sea, and enrolled the Tyrrhenians in a vast army which was meant to conquer Egypt. If there had been " forced " soldiers among the Northmen then they could not have been Denes, but Sardanas and Sekelese.

## 6. CONCLUSIONS

The results of the investigation in the last chapter can be summed up as follows: the statements of the Atlantis report and the contemporary Egyptian inscriptions and papyri, that the Atlanteans or North Sea people originate from the

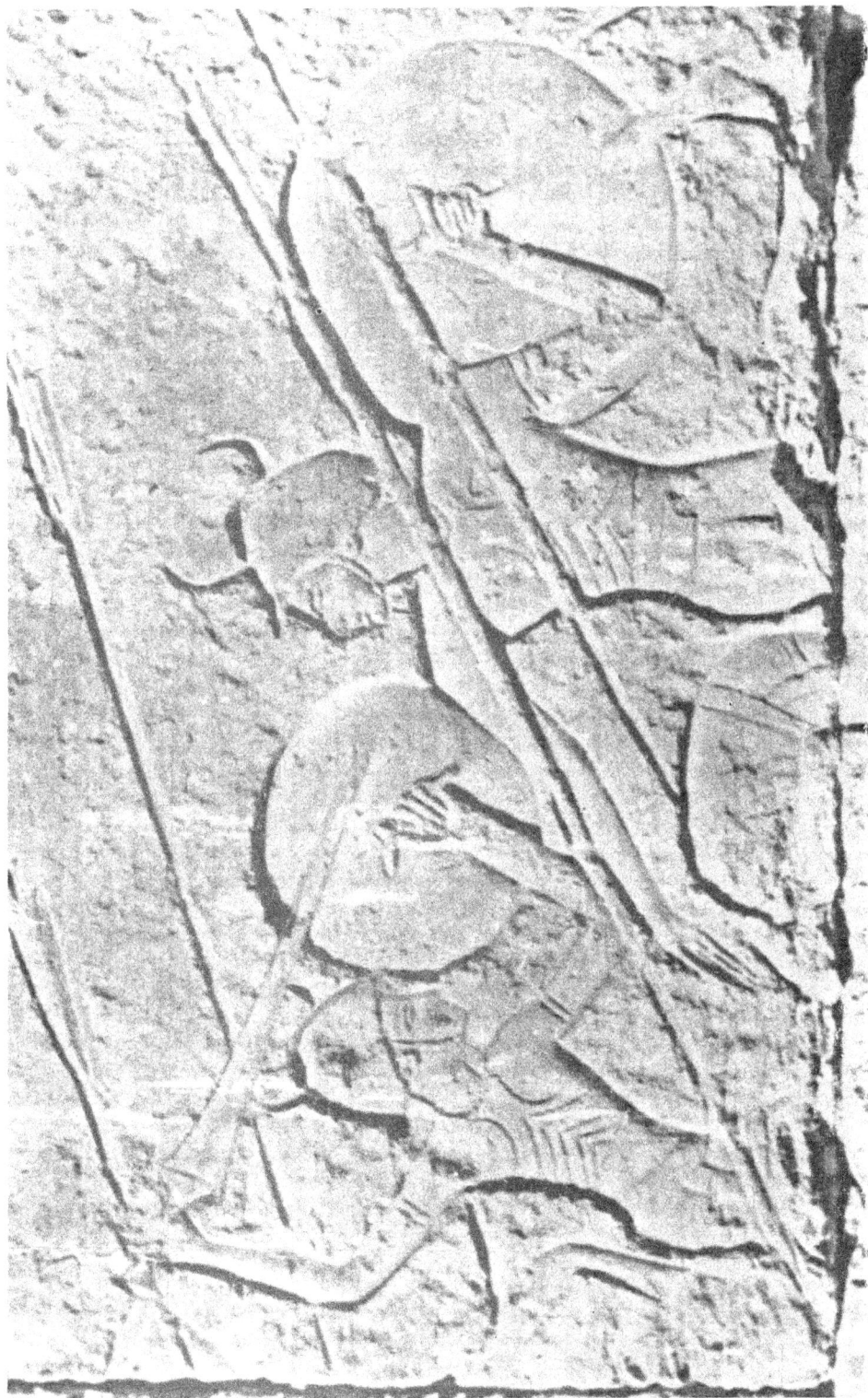

Two North people wearing horn helmets on board a Northern ship.

Northern prisoners on board an Egyptian warship.

World Sea in the North, correspond without doubt to actual historical facts.

The archæological material confirms the accuracy of the Egyptian statements and certifies the origin of these people from the North Sea area. A gigantic migration from these territories towards the end of the thirteenth century B.C. is proved by archæological research.

We are therefore compelled to look in the North Sea area for Atlantis, the main island, upon which stood the royal fortress of the Atlantis kingdom, called for that reason " Basileia," or " Chief of Cities."

## THE SITE OF THE ROYAL ISLE BASILEIA

THE following details are at our disposal if we want to determine the exact position of the chief, or Royal, Isle of Atlantis:

1. Immediately in front of Basileia lay a stretch of land, also called "island," which has been described as being very high, and rising from the sea as if cut off by a knife. This island consisted of red, white and black stone which was used by the Atlanteans for building walls and houses.

2. Basileia itself was situated immediately behind the rock island towards the mainland, from which it was separated only by a narrow stretch of sea. The royal isle had a radius of only fifty stadiens—about six miles—and was an incredibly fertile plain, surrounded by low hills along the sea-front. In the centre of the royal isle, six miles from the sea, was a low hill upon which were erected the royal fortress and the temple of Poseidon.

3. After the fall of the royal isle the area in which it was situated was turned into a sea of mud, which, according to Plato, was made impassable and impenetrable by the vast mass of mud which lay on the sinking isle.

4. In many parts of the island Orichalc was dug out of the ground.

5. Copper in fusible and pure state was found on the island.

### I.   THE ROCK ISLAND BEFORE BASILEIA

In the whole range of the North Sea there is only one rock island which rises high above the sea, cut off like a knife, and which consists of red, white and black stone: the rock island of Heligoland.

The red rock of this island still exists nowadays. The white rock consisted of plaster, chalk and shellfish chalk and was situated where the " Dunes " are today and still forms part of its bottom base. In historical times these rocks were of about the same height, like the part of the island remaining today. As shown by the sea map, it stretched in a large radius around the so-called " South Harbour " southwards, and in gigantic runners to the north. The black rock is still found in shallow depth in the northern extension of the dunes. It is actually sandstone, well impregnated with calcium carbonate copper, which produces its blue-black to black colour. Apart from the sea, which reached Heligoland about 5000 B.C., man contributed to the destruction of the white as well as the black rock. Plaster of Paris and chalk were, until 230 years ago much-sought-after building materials. Up to 200 ships were said to have anchored at the same time in the South Harbour to carry away the plaster of this rock. But 230 years ago the remaining part of the chalk massif crashed into the sea in a great storm.

## 2.   THE CASTLE HILL OF BASILEIA

The main island of the Atlantis kingdom, also called Basileia, was, according to the Atlantis report, situated behind the rock island, towards the mainland. It was said of Basileia that near the centre of the island was a plain which reached the sea and which was very fertile and beautiful. In the centre of this plain, six miles from the sea, was a low hill, upon which stood the royal castle which gave the island its name, as well as the temple of Poseidon. This building and the wall on the royal hill was made of stones, red, white and black, which were broken by the Atlanteans on the nearby rock island.

Indeed, exactly six miles distant from Heligoland in the direction of the mainland can be found a hill which rises about twenty-one feet above sea level. This hill is strewn with large stones and is therefore called " Stoneground " (Steingrund). According to an ancient Heligoland legend there once stood on this hill a temple and a castle. According

to the Atlantis report this must be the spot where stood the
royal castle and the temple of Poseidon.

We must ask the question whether there did in fact exist
a royal castle, or an island called Basileia, and, if so, can it
have existed around 1200 B.C.?

At about 350 B.C. the rich merchant Pytheas of Massilia
undertook a research expedition into the North Sea area. He
reached the Watten Sea, near the west coast of Schleswig-
Holstein, which he is said to have seen with his own eyes.
Unfortunately Pytheas' report has been lost, but we are able
to reconstruct some of his accounts on the basis of quotations
of ancient writers. Diodorus of Sicily reports that opposite
Scythia, his name for Germany, lay an island which was
called Basileia. There the waves wash against amber, which
does not appear in any other part of the world. Diodorus
then relates the fable of Phæthon, which we have already
heard from the mouth of the Egyptian priests. He related
how Phæthon's sisters wept tears beside the Eridanus for
their brother who was hurled from heaven. These tears are
said to have changed into amber and were then carried by the
River Eridanus to the island of Basileia. Thus the island
Basileia must have been situated in the amber district.

As we have already emphasised, it is of no importance
whether we identify Eridanus with the River Elbe or the
River Eider. The district in question lies near the mouth of
both rivers. But as even today the River Eider, but not the
Elbe, contains amber, particularly near its mouth, we shall
identify Eridanus with Eider.

For geological reasons amber is not to be found on the
Heligoland chalk and coloured sandstone massif. The amber
island Basileia must therefore have been situated between
Heligoland and the island at the mouth of the River Eider.
Without doubt the Basileia island of the Atlantis report is
identical with the island mentioned by Pytheas, Diodorus
and Pliny. Both islands bear the same name and are placed
on the same spot, and both stood in the mud at the mouth of
the River Eider. We are told, however, that the Basileia of
the Atlantis report was destroyed around 1200 B.C. during a
period of gigantic earthquakes and floods. Is it possible that

an island which perished around 1200 B.C. could have become visible again at 400 B.C. and during the following centuries?

The latest investigations have shown that the main causes for the after-glacial coast shifts were to be found in the eustatic water-level variations. The theory of Eustasia says: The height of sea level is dependent on the ice masses of all glacier-formation territories of the water mass of the earth. Warm climatic periods cause the ice masses of the earth to melt and thereby cause a rise in sea level (transgression), whilst cold climatic periods bind the water mass in the glacier-formation territories, causing a lowering of the sea level (regression). In our context this means that the sea reached its highest level at the end of the Bronze Age, which ended in a terrible period of heat which caused the glaciers to be pushed far back to their present-day positions, whilst it reached its lowest point during the Iron Age, which was marked by a world-wide lowering of temperature. Schutte has determined that the transition from the highest to the lowest level took place around 1100 B.C., and has estimated that the drop in sea level during the Iron Age from the highest level was about twelve feet.

All territories, therefore, which lay twelve feet under the sea at the end of the Bronze Age must have appeared again above sea level with the regression of the Iron Age. Peculiar circumstances were connected with Basileia: in the centre of the island was a hill which rose above the other land. This hill was not submerged by the normal eustatic rising of the sea level, but through a catastrophic coincidence of earth-quake, storm and floods.

Such a coincidence of earthquake, storm and floods has also been noticed on the German west coast in A.D. 1634, when the dikes were submerged, settlements destroyed and large stretches of land turned into a sea of mud. After the storms subsided these submerged parts appeared once more and were again inhabited.

Similar conditions must have prevailed during the sinking of Basileia. Although the flat part of Basileia was destroyed and flooded through the catastrophes of those days, the royal hill only became submerged through the most severe floods; after these subsided the hill must have been visible again. When during the next centuries the sea level sank by more than twelve feet through the regression of the Iron Age, the hill was without doubt habitable again and became a centre of the amber trade in the North Sea.

There can be no doubt, therefore, that this hill of Basileia, which in 1200 B.C. stood several yards above sea level, could again have been walked upon in the fourth century B.C. by Pytheas. This fact, which has been proved through geology and oceanography, is confirmed by an ancient Greek legend which says that where Atlantis had once sunk, seven smaller and three larger islands later appeared. The inhabitants of these islands are said to have kept the memories handed down to them by their ancestors that a large island once stood in the vicinity and for many centuries ruled over all the islands of the outer sea. The Greek historian Marcellus has handed down this legend, referring to the oldest historical writers, and it is therefore older than the Atlantis report of Plato and independent of it.

We do not know the actual time when Basileia became submerged. Pytheas of Massilia set foot on the remains of Basileia, in 350 B.C., and it is later mentioned by Metrodorus Scepsius (150 B.C.), by Xenophon of Lampsacus (100 B.C.), by Diodorus of Sicily (50 B.C.) and Pliny (50 B.C.).

A good deal can be said in favour of the theory that this remaining part of Basileia is identical with Fosites Land, the holy island of the Firsians. On Fosites Land the evangelists Wulfram, Willibrod and Ludger proclaimed the Christian message. In the biographies of these three missionaries we learn many details about the island.

The following facts prove the identity of Fosites Land with that of Basileia: both islands were undoubtedly situated in front of the west coast of Schleswig-Holstein, both had a central temple and a royal castle. Both islands also possessed a sacred spring near which holy animals grazed. Basileia was dedicated to Poseidon and Fosites Land to the Fosites. In all probability Poseidon and Fosites are in their essence and names identical. In ancient Dorian Poseidon is also

called " Posides," a name which is similar to the Frisian
name " Fosites." We learn about Poseidon and Fosites that
they lived in the amber temple and that they ruled the sea,
made laws and protected the rights.

Adam of Bremen (A.D. 1075) was the first to identify
Fosites Land with Heligoland. Many scholars have since
agreed with him. For a number of reasons Fosites Land
cannot be identified with the rock island of Heligoland,
but it is possible that it is identical with Basileia, the " Holy
Island " which once stood to the east of Heligoland.
Geologists, however, emphasise that during the time of
Christian conversion—in the seventh and eighth centuries—
no islands could have been situated to the east of Heligoland.
Against the view of the geologists speaks the ancient Frisian
legend, which maintains that the last remains of " Holy

Drawing after the oldest extant map of Heligoland, dating from around A.D. 1570.
Schleswig Museum.

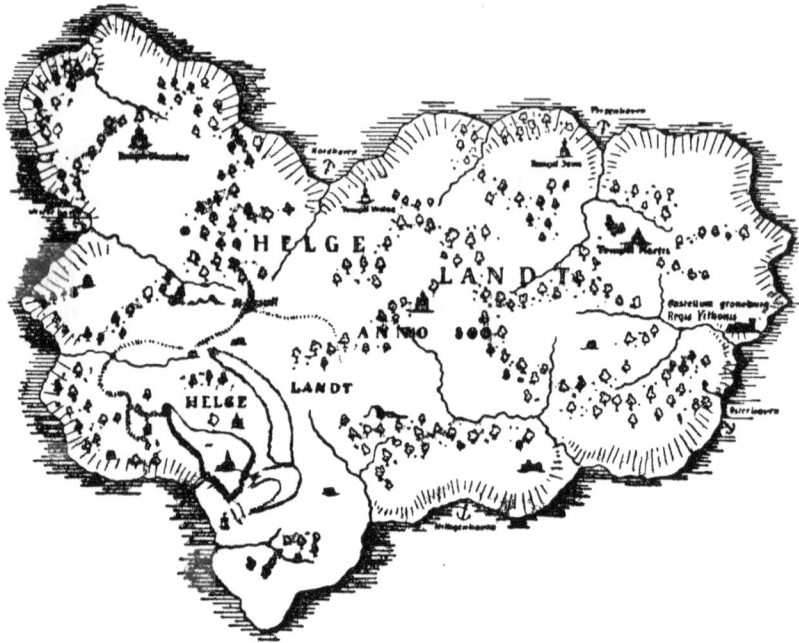

Map of Heligoland made by Johannes Meyer in 1650 based on old
fables and tradition.

Land," as this island was called during the Middle Ages,
perished only in 1216. Whether the geologists or the North
Frisian is correct can only be confirmed by a close examination of the stone ground. On the oldest map of Heligoland,
dating back to 1570, to the east of Heligoland is marked
" Steinwirk ", upon which seven churches are said to have
stood. On another map, dated 1650, there is marked in the
vicinity of the stone ground a temple and a castle. The
Frisian chronicler Heimriech mentions forests, temples and
castles which once stood to the east of Heligoland, and he
adds that the residence and court of the first kings of the
country were situated there.

Even today the " Holy Island " lives in the legends of the
Heligoland inhabitants, and in the name carried by the
remaining rock which has survived the catastrophes: Holy
Land, or Heligoland.

### 3.  THE SEA OF MUD

In the Atlantis report Plato relates that after the fall of Atlantis the place which was occupied by the island was turned into a sea of mud. It says in the *Dialogues*: " This island has sunk into the sea through earthquakes, and anyone intending to reach the sea on the other side will be prevented by the hindering mass of mud."

How did Plato know that the stretch of sea around Basileia was impassable and impenetrable during his time?

Shortly before Plato's death and the writing of the *Dialogues* of Critias, Pytheas returned from his expedition to the amber territory. He reported that the sea area around Basileia consisted of a mixture of water, mud and air and could be compared with a sea-lung. He said that he saw the area himself and that it was neither passable nor penetrable.

Plato may have known of these reports of Pytheas, and could then have had every right to quote the assertion of an eye-witness that the area around Basileia was neither passable nor penetrable. Where there once were fertile plains, during the Iron Age, there were tremendous shallow stretches of mud. Out of these seas of mud only the old royal hill appeared; it may have been similar to the Watten Sea of today, where at low tide traces of cultures, remains of settlements and even furrows of fields are visible.

A further proof of the identity of the island of Basileia of the Atlantis report with the island of Basileia of Pytheas is the statement made above that by the sinking of Basileia the path to the outer sea became blocked, so that anyone who wanted to cross to the sea was prevented by the mass of mud which confronted him. Without doubt this is a reference to the Eider trench way, the ancient route from the North to the Baltic Sea. An island, the sinking of which could block this channel, could only have been situated at the mouth of the River Eider. The same is said by Diodorus in the Pytheas report about the position of the island Basileia which was also situated at the mouth of the River Eridanus, or Eider.

In fact this Eider trench way, as shown by numerous pre-

historic finds and burial grounds along its banks, was already
in use during the beginning of the Bronze Age. In those days
the River Eider ran without hindrance towards the west and,
forming the southern border of the island Basileia, into the
North Sea. The course of the Eider was blocked by the
climatic catastrophes. The sea threw up an enormous
" beach wall," the so-called Lundenberger Sand. This
narrow tongue of land was a wall twelve miles long and up
to twenty feet high running from south to north across the
former course of the River Eider. This river was diverted
northwards by the gigantic beach wall and the opening of
the river mouth was choked with mud; the way from Basileia
to the outer sea was blocked.


### 4.   ORICHALC

A further proof of the position of Basileia-Atlantis and of
the identification of this island with the Basileia of Pytheas is
provided by the details of the Atlantis report regarding
orichalc. Although it has always been difficult to ascertain
what kind of material orichalc was, the problem has now
been solved.

The Atlantis report relates the following about the
mysterious orichalc. This material, which is known today
only by its name, orichalc, was found in many parts of the
island, and was valued by the people of the time as highly as
gold. They decorated the crest of the outer dikes with
orichalc by covering them with oil. The crest of the inside
wall was also decorated with orichalc, which possessed a
fiery gloss. As far as the interior of the temple was concerned,
the ceiling was decorated with gold, ebony, silver and
orichalc, and the rest—walls, columns and floors—was
covered with orichalc.

Many scholars have attempted to solve the riddle of
orichalc. Some of these have assumed, as Plato mentions
orichalc after speaking about copper, which was widely used
in Basileia, that it was a kind of metal. These scholars
believed Atlantis to have been rich in metals. Other
scholars claim to see in the legend of orichalc a typical

fairy-tale element, and have therefore banished the whole history of Atlantis into the land of fable.

Orichalc has therefore become a basic problem in any research into Atlantis. It has become evident that the whole problem of Atlantis is dependent on its solution. The following theories about the existence of this material have been put forward. Most of the investigators have translated the word orichalc with bronze copper metal, because they are of the opinion that orichalc was an alloy of gold and copper. This view is in contradiction to the express statements of the Atlantis report that orichalc was dug out of the earth in many parts of the island. It was therefore a natural product and not an artificial alloy. An alloy of gold and copper cannot be applied with oil, to be used as a coat of paint on walls and columns.

The Atlantis scholar Netolitzky believes that it was an alloy of copper and silver. For this reason Atlantis must have been situated in the neighbourhood of Tartesses, where both metals were to be found in abundance. But silver copper is also an artificial alloy and not a natural product. It cannot be dug out of the ground, nor can it be made fluid with oil for painting purposes. The Munich professor Borchardt is of the opinion that orichalc was an alloy of copper and zinc, a kind of brass, a theory also expressed by the Dutch historian Hermann Wirt. Finally we must mention the strange suggestion of the Russian Mereshkowsky, who believes that orichalc was a metal peculiar to Atlantis which later disappeared from Nature. No wonder that serious scholars who know these attempts to solve the orichalc problem reject the whole Atlantis report. And yet, all these scholars could have easily found out the substance of orichalc by looking into the graves of the Bronze Age in order to find out which pieces of decoration amongst those people had, next to gold, the highest value. They would have seen that, apart from the rich finds of gold, amber was often to be found as a highly valued piece of decoration. From Egypt, Crete, Asia Minor and Mycenæa, over Spain, Northern France, Ireland, England, Northern Germany to Denmark and Southern Sweden, amber decorations and ornaments were often found in the graves of the Bronze Age. The orichalc of the Atlantis report could only mean amber, and we shall therefore translate the word orichalc with amber.

All statements of the Atlantis report concerning orichalc apply to amber, and amber alone. There are in fact kinds of amber which show a " fiery gloss." Apart from gold, amber was valued highest; it can be cooked in oil and be used as " amber varnish " for painting walls. An amber ring of the size of a crown piece, which, together with bronze articles and gold rings, was found in a Bronze Age grave on the North German island of Sylt, is proof that the inhabitants of the North Sea islands already knew this technique during the Bronze Age. Tacitus mentions the liquefaction of amber by heating, and Pliny reports that the North Sea people used amber for heating instead of wood.

They evidently knew how to colour amber by cooking it in honey and coloured oil. As reported in the Atlantis legend, it was certainly used to decorate the temples. There are different reports about the decoration of Egyptian temples with Nordic amber. Homer had remarkably exact knowledge of Basileia, and he mentions that the temple of the greatest god glittered with gold, amber, ebony and silver. According to Pliny, the Teutons called amber " glæsum," and the amber islands in the North Sea are called " glæsariæ " by him. The word " glass " is an ancient Nordic word for amber. In the days of Pytheas Basileia was the main amber island, and Diodorus even reports amber is not found anywhere in the world except on Basileia. After its final destruction, the amber temple of Atlantis passed into the legends of the Nordic people as " glass castle," " glass tower," and the sunken amber island Basileia became the Island of the Dead, and was called " Glass Mountain." We shall hear more about these legends later on. For the moment the important fact is that the sunken highest shrine of the Northern area was called Glass Mountain, or Glass Tower, which proves that for all these legends an amber temple was set as an example. We have therefore put our trust in the statements of the Atlantis report, that the main temple on Atlantis-Basileia was lavishly decorated with amber.

The orichalc, which until now was the most important evidence for the fabulousness of the Atlantis report, is in reality an important proof of the historical reliability of the original Atlantis report, and at the same time a convincing affirmation for the position of Basileia-Atlantis near Heligoland, and for the identification of the Basileia of the Atlantis report with the Basileia of Pytheas.

### 5.   AMBER

Until today only two amber deposits are known on the earth, one in the Samland and the other on the west coast of the Cymbrian peninsula.  There are deposits of fossil resin, which is akin to amber, as, for example, in Spain, Italy, Sicily and in Transylvania, but these fossil resins are distinguished from amber by their lack of amber acid which amounts to 3 to 8 per cent. in Nordic amber.  Nordic amber can be easily distinguished from fossil resin by chemical analysis.

Nordic amber has been found in Egyptian graves of the sixth dynasty, as early as 2500 B.C. It has also been found in Spain, Northern France, Ireland, England and in the whole of the Nordic area in megalith graves and in grave hills of the Bronze Age between 3000–2000 B.C.  The pit graves of Mycæna during the period 1500–1200 B.C. were especially rich in Nordic amber.

The Egyptians knew at least since Thutmose III (1500 B.C.) that amber came from the farthest North.  The Greeks also knew that amber originated from the Northern Sea. Herodotus wrote: " There is a river, called Eridanus by the barbarians, which flows into the Northern Ocean, and the amber comes from there." We have already heard of the reports of Pytheas, Diodorus, Timæus, etc., regarding the amber island in the North Sea.  Pliny also leaves no doubt that the " glæsariæ " can be found in the Northern Ocean, and not in the Baltic Sea.

Although these ancient reports about the origin of amber at the time before the birth of Christ are completely clear, it was thought until sixty to seventy years ago that the Samland was the amber land of ancient times.  Only gradually was it

realised that while the Samland was the main supply country
of amber since Roman times, in earlier times, particularly
during the Bronze Age, the west coast of Schleswig-Holstein
was the only amber country. For a long time Heligoland
was thought to have been the amber island of the ancients.
But geological investigations of E. Wasmunds have shown
that there could not have been any amber on Heligoland,
because the geological conditions for its occurrence are
absent from the multi-coloured sandstone and chalk. He
asserts that Basileia, the amber island proper, must have sunk
into the sea, and he put the island outside the south-west
coast of Eiderstedt. Hennig believes the island to have been
half-way between Heligoland and Eiderstedt. These
scholars were looking for the amber island Basileia just where
the orichalc island of the Atlantis report was situated.

There is hardly a better proof for the reliability of the
Atlantis report than the exact position of the orichalc-amber
island of Basileia which is given exactly where geological and
archæological investigations of our time have shown it to be.

### 6.  COPPER ON BASILEIA

It is altogether remarkable what the Atlantis report says
about the great wealth of copper on Basileia. It even
maintains that this metal was produced there in solid as
well as in fusible form.

For a long time it was forgotten that there had been copper
on Heligoland, although eminent geologists have repeatedly
mentioned it. According to the investigations of the geologist
Bolton, the whole stone massif of the island of Heligoland
was impregnated with copper carbonate. Even more
remarkable than the presence of copper in the white, green
and red layers of the multi-coloured sandstone is that found
in the north-east of the island. There sandstone can be found
which is richly impregnated with carbonic acid copper. On
the surface of the stone the copper carbonate was changed
into multi-coloured and red copper metal which engulfed
small pieces of solid copper. Solid copper of the size of peas
has often been found, and the chemist Hoffman has even

found two pieces weighing eight to twelve ounces. Spectro-analytical investigations of solid copper pieces from Heligoland have shown that it was extremely pure copper.

According to the geologist Schreiter the presence of this copper was already known to the people of antiquity. In the Bronze Age the Northmen possessed considerable metallurgic skill and a complete mastery of metal technique which was based on copper. Their capital was situated in the immediate vicinity of these copper treasures and it is unlikely that they would not have used this copper field. When the Atlantis report says that the inhabitants of Basileia found on their island pure and fusible copper, then this means without doubt that copper was to be found on Heligoland during the Bronze Age.

A strange sentence in the Atlantis report may perhaps be an indication of how the inhabitants of Basileia, that is the Atlanteans, brought about the mining of the copper deposits on Heligoland. It is said that they broke the stone of the rock island around the shores and in the centre of the island, thereby creating caves and ships' bunkers which were covered by rock.

It is improbable that the men of Basileia broke these enormous masses of rock purely to build walls and temples. Furthermore, the difficult structure of caves for the accom-modation of ships was by no means necessary. The Atlanteans possessed a good number of excellent harbours within the ring dikes, and did not really need these bunkers. But as copper was deposited to a large extent in the caves and shores of the island, the copper yield must have been most successful in these places. It is most probable that the stone was broken for the purpose of copper extraction. Natural caves were enlarged and could be used as ships' bunkers when they were level with the sea.

Witter and Otto have proved without doubt that solid copper was used in prehistoric metallurgy. At first solid, or pure copper, was used. Only later came the working of oxydised metal by reduction means, and later still the working of sulphide metals. Pure copper is difficult to melt, because its melting point is as high as wrought-iron. For this reason pure copper was first worked by hammering. It is possible that it only became known in the later Bronze Age that pure copper can also be melted down. A great amount of the bronze articles of that time consisted of zinc bronze with a content of eighty-six per cent. pure copper, a further proof that this technique was known during the Bronze Age.

The origin of the pure copper of the earliest metal age and Bronze Age has hitherto been a puzzle. It was believed that Hungarian copper deposits were the chief sources. Is it not possible that the deposits of Heligoland, which contained extremely pure copper, were also sources? Articles of pure copper were found in the great stone graves of the North Sea area, which is an indication that the oldest copper originated in Nordic as well as Hungarian deposits. We cannot believe that the large masses of pure copper, which during the Bronze Age was mainly used for the making of zinc bronze, were all imported from Hungary. If this was the case then large quantities of Nordic barter articles, for example amber, must have been found in Hungary, which is not so. For the manufacture of their zinc bronze the Norsemen mainly used pure copper and the oxydised copper metals of Heligoland. This is the only explanation for the enormous quarries which were being worked in Heligoland during the Bronze Age.

It is probably an exaggeration when it is said in the Atlantis report that the walls of the royal city were decorated with copper. This exaggeration can probably be ascribed to the Norsemen themselves, and not to Plato or Solon. Even nowadays the legend exists that the fabulously rich town near Heligoland possessed canals made of copper.

In conclusion we can confirm that the statement of the Atlantis report that the inhabitants of Basileia worked copper, which was abundant on their island, in pure and fusible form was based on facts. As pure copper, copper metal and amber appeared together nowhere else in the world, the exact locality of Basileia-Atlantis in the immediate vicinity of Heligoland is undoubtedly correct. The great wealth which, according to the Atlantis report, prevailed in Basileia, can be attributed largely to the town's world-wide commerce in amber and copper.

Fallen Northern warrior wearing a reed crown.

Two Northern warriors with horn helmets in the sea battle with the Egyptians.

### 7. THE GOLD, SILVER AND ZINC TREASURE OF THE ATLANTEANS

According to the Atlantis report, the Atlanteans are said to have owned a great quantity of gold, silver and zinc. The statement regarding the quantity of these metals is probably an exaggeration. Golden walls in the temple and gold statues of gods hardly existed in the North. But we have to investigate further the question whether the Norsemen during the Bronze Age really did dispose of great wealth, and, if so, where did it come from?

Much has been written about the astonishing wealth of gold and zinc which was to be found in Nordic parts during the earlier Bronze Age. Schilling speaks of really fantastic masses of gold which, together with bronze, were carried towards the North. He says that during the early Stone Age this metal was as good as non-existent. At the beginning of the trade in amber it became almost common in the North. The simplest spiral finger ring, made of gold wire, which at first was used as means of exchange in the North, was so frequent that every Teutonic girl must have owned one. When we consider that finds of gold have always been exposed to the greed of the finders and were seldom, if ever, handed over, then the wealth of gold of the Norsemen must have been immeasurable. Conservative estimates, based on the pieces which are now in museums, put these as no more than one-half per cent. of the valuables originally deposited in burial places and elsewhere; it has been calculated that for Denmark alone the value of gold corresponds to that of £13 million. How great the total wealth of the Teutons must have been when these valuables were presented to the dead and the gods alone! A comparison with the Nordic finds can only be found in the ancient graves and treasure chambers of the Egyptian and Mesopotamian rulers, but it has to be remembered that nearly all the precious metal of the latter countries was concentrated in one place, whilst in the North, in contrast, every free person must have owned considerable wealth. We come to similar results when we consider that the means of barter, through which the Teutons obtained gold and bronze, must have been an unending source of wealth. The finds of North Sea amber became exhausted before the turn of the age, but we cannot assume that during the Bronze Age the total annual yield was much less than that of today, as amber fishing on the German Baltic Sea coast was carried out by old and primitive methods.

L. Meyn has calculated that on the west coast of the Cymbrian peninsula, during the time of the Romans, about 6,000,000 pounds of amber was collected. It is obvious that amber deposits during the time when amber could be collected in many places along that coast must have been much larger.

There is no doubt that the amber trade was a source of great wealth in the North. Schwantes speaks about the extraordinary gold treasures which were owned by Nordic peasants, and points out that during the Bronze Age the coastal and island settlements of the North Sea flourished and enjoyed great prosperity.

Everything points to the fact that on the main island of these territories, where the largest amber deposits were situated and whence they were transported to destinations the world over, wealth was in abundance. The ancient Frisian legend tells of the unbelievable wealth of this " golden town ": the inhabitants were so rich that they shod their horses with golden horse-shoes, and cultivated their land with silver plough-shares.

Traces of silver can be found mainly in Bronze Age alloys, such as silver bronze with a content of two per cent. silver. Silver evidently did not enjoy the same popularity in the North as gold. It is possible that the inhabitants of Basileia when extracting copper found silver, as this was also available on the island.

The Norse people also possessed a large quantity of zinc. It was added to melting copper, in a mixture of up to fourteen per cent. In this way the highly valued zinc bronze was produced, which was used almost exclusively in the North during the Bronze Age.

According to the general belief of scholars, gold and zinc were transported into the North mainly from Ireland. The historian Stroebel says that Jutlandic amber is very frequent in the districts of the bowl graves of England and Northern Ireland, where it was used for making pearls and accessories. Irish gold collars have often been found in Northern Spain, as well as in Brittany, North-West Germany and Denmark. In some cases Irish gold arm rings were introduced into North-West Germany. Small sun discs made of gold tin found their way with other small gold articles in the first period of the Bronze Age from Ireland to Brittany and Germany. During the second period the Teutons made their own wonderful sun discs out of Irish gold.

The statements of the Atlantis report about the great wealth of gold, silver and copper can therefore withstand critical examination. Apart from small exaggerations which are not Plato's fault, these statements correspond to the actual conditions during the Bronze Age in the Nordic territories.

The mention of ivory, which is said to have been used for the decoration of the temple of the highest god, also corresponds to the actual facts. We shall see later on that another source, independent of the Atlantis report, mentions ivory as decoration and ornamentation on Basileia.

Two kinds of ivory can be distinguished: African ivory, which comes from the tusks of elephants, and Nordic ivory, from the tusks of walruses, narwhals and fossilised mammoth skeletons. Numerous mammoth bones have been found in the Nordic area. Over two thousand back teeth of mammoths alone have been " fished up " within a dozen years from the Dogger Bank. In a part of Northern Germany the skeleton of an ancient elephant was recently found which still had an eight-feet-long spear between its ribs. The Norse people were therefore not dependent on the importation of ivory from Africa, although there is also African ivory in the North. During the Middle Ages it was reported by the Norwegian Otter, who lived in the ninth century A.D., that walrus tusks were a much used article of export from the Nordic area.

It is possible that the false statement of the Egyptian priests, that there had been elephants during the Bronze Age in the Atlantis region, originated from the knowledge that ivory treasures were hidden in the temple of Poseidon. For the Egyptians there was only one animal which carried ivory, the elephant. This error could also have been due to the fact that Libyan and Norse prisoners were interrogated together, as is shown in the great relief of Medinet Habu. In the Libya of those days there were still large herds of elephants, as many rock drawings and numerous finds reveal. Since the Libyans were thought to be North people, this must have been the cause of the erroneous belief that there were elephants in the Nordic areas.

### 8.   IRON ON ATLANTIS

It is related in the Atlantis report that the Atlanteans also knew iron, but that iron implements were not allowed to be used in the ceremonial bull-fights. Does this statement correspond with the facts?

According to the thorough investigations of W. Witters there is no doubt that the North people, during their invasion of the South-Eastern territories, had already mastered the technique of iron tool production. In the graves of Philistines of that age we can always find weapons made of iron, besides those made of bronze. According to Old Testament sources we learn that the Philistines in the eleventh century B.C. carried out an iron production monopoly, and even knew how to make steel. Witter maintains that at least some of the North people must have known the iron technique before the start of the Great Migration. During the migration itself the North people would not have been able to acquire the knowledge of iron production, as, on the one hand, the peoples they came across did not know how to produce iron at that time, and, on the other, a migrating race, continually exposed to the hazards of war, could not have mastered the metallurgy of iron, or acquired the necessary experience in iron production for making weapons and tools. Witter is convinced that the North people had centuries-old experience in the melting of metals and the forging of copper and bronze, as the reduction of iron could only have been carried out by experienced metal experts.

We know now that these people came from the North Sea

area, and that they left their homes in the second half of the thirteenth century B.C. Are there indications that the manufacture of iron implements was already known at that time in the Nordic area? According to Witters, iron tools were already known in the Nordic area from the fourteenth century B.C.; on a grave hill in Zealand, apart from relics of clothing, a piece of iron was found, and on a grave hill on Bornholm, in addition to bronze articles, an iron knife-blade was found. In the second part of the thirteenth century B.C., the period covered in the Atlantis report, the Nordic area was undergoing Period IV of the Bronze Age. From this period comes a razor found in Northern Germany, on which is represented in gold a ship, whilst the waves are indicated in iron. This find proves that in the Northern area iron was not only known, but that the difficult technique of inlaid iron had already been mastered. It also suggests that iron was seldom used during that period.

During Period V iron appeared in the North much more frequently. Particularly remarkable is an arched knife with a bronze grip, and a partially destroyed blade of iron, which was found with a similar knife with a bronze blade in a grave in Holstein, Northern Germany. The iron finds of this Period V show that this metal was used more widely, but they also prove that in the North the art of making iron tools had been completely mastered, a technique, which according to Witter, took several centuries to develop.

As the manufacture of pure copper into zinc bronze shows, the Norse people in the earlier Bronze Age knew how to produce temperatures at which forged iron and pure copper would melt. As the stone of Heligoland contains, apart from copper, a large degree of iron, the Norse people must have acquired a knowledge of iron when they melted copper.

The statement of the Atlantis report that the Atlanteans had knowledge of iron corresponds without doubt to the facts. Perhaps the saying of Æschylus, that the North country at the ends of the earth is the mother country of iron—like the words of Jeremiah: " Iron and metal from the land of midnight "—is a reminder of the origin of the first iron and the first iron experts from the North lands.

## THE SIZE AND ORGANISATION
## OF THE ATLANTEAN EMPIRE

### I.   THE SIZE OF THE ATLANTEAN KINGDOM

THE Atlantis report says about the size of the Atlantean kingdom that it stretched over many islands and parts of the mainland. The length on one side covered about four hundred miles. From the sea to the centre the distance was about two hundred miles, and this side of the kingdom stretched from north to south.

The term " centre " was often used in the Atlantis report to describe the main island Basileia, because this was the political and religious centre of the Atlantean kingdom. The above statement must therefore read as follows: from the sea in the north to the capital southwards the distance was two hundred miles, and in another direction, from west to east, the Atlantean kingdom covered four hundred miles.

Are these statements based on historical facts, or is it all fantasy?

If we measure two hundred miles north from Basileia, we reach almost exactly the north side of the Jutland Bank, the Skagerrak, which is evidently the " Sea in the North." As in those days a number of islands were situated around the Amrum and Jutland Banks, the report is correct when it says that it was only possible to reach the open sea northwards from Basileia after walking two hundred miles.

Four hundred miles in an eastern direction from Basileia comprises an area which includes the Danish islands, Southern Sweden, and the island of Oeland. According to the statements of the Atlantis report, the following areas must have belonged to the Atlantean kingdom during the

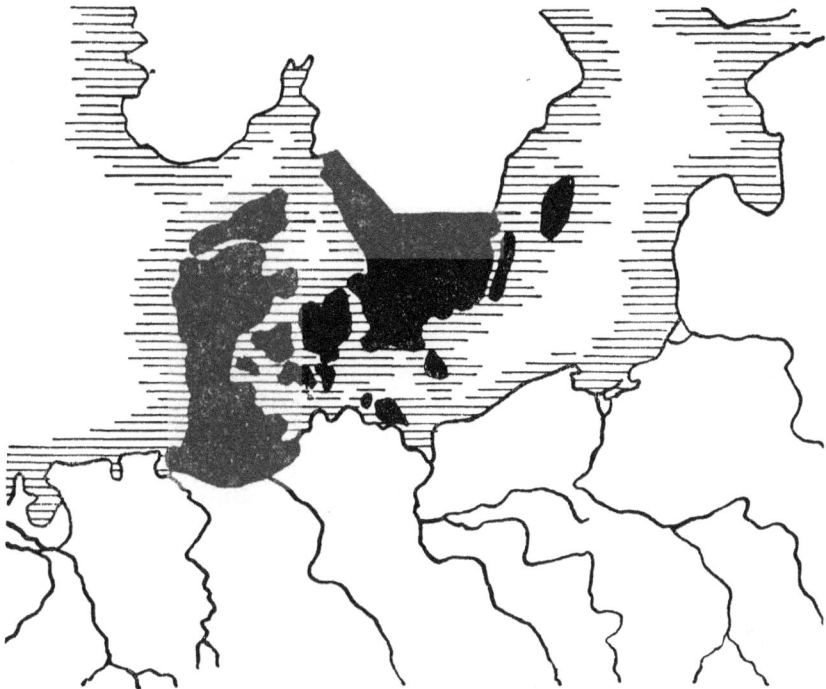

Map of the area of the Northern culture—the Kingdom of the Atlanteans
in the 13th century B.C.

Bronze Age: the whole of the Cymbrian peninsula and the
islands to the west of it, the Danish islands, Southern Sweden
and Oeland.

Is this statement feasible?

Exactly in the parts described a culture flourished during
the Bronze Age which, in prehistoric research, is known
as " singularly unique." The area of this culture is described
as the " Nordic Circle." As shown by Kersten, three
different cultural zones can be indicated within the Nordic
circle; but taken together the finds from the area between
the North Sea islands and Southern Sweden give the
impression of a unified, self-contained cultural zone. The
cultural unity of this area has been confirmed by prehistory.
But the Atlantis report also maintains that this area was an
entity from a political and religious point of view. Is this

within the realm of possibility? Archæological finds certainly cannot give us an answer, but perhaps the report itself will provide further help.

## 2. ITS ORGANISATION

In the *Dialogues* of Critias the following is said about the constitution and organisation of the Atlantean kingdom: " Concerning the number of inhabitants, the regulation existed that every district in the plain had to provide a leader from the able-bodied male population; the size of a district amounted to 100 landless people or ' hinds.' The total number of these forces amounted to 60,000 men. According to the laws, the leaders had to provide a war chariot for six men, so that there were 10,000 chariots, and in addition to the horses and riders, a two-horsed team without a chariot which was manned by a warrior who carried a small shield and fought on foot. Furthermore, each leader had to provide two heavily armed warriors, two bowmen, one stone- and spear-thrower without armour, and finally four sailors for the crews of the 1,200 ships."

This description of the organisation of the Atlantean kingdom—division of the area into landless persons, inclusion of 100 hinds in one district under one leader, a force of 100 soldiers from six collective districts—corresponds in a remarkable degree to the organisation found in the Nordic area from the Frisian islands to Oeland. Originally it was believed that the smallest departmental unit was the " hide," a hundred of which comprised a larger unit. It was assumed from this that in the Nordic area every hide had to supply one man in case of war, and that every larger unit, called " hundari," had to supply a hundred men. Further investigations, however, have shown that this view is untenable. It was shown that the " hundari " were not military but commercial units. The same interpretation is expressed in the Atlantis report. According to this the smallest departmental unit was not a military but an economic unit. Every hundred " hides " formed the next highest unit, called a " cleros " in the Atlantis report.

Is it possible that this departmental unit system already existed in the Nordic area in the Bronze Age?

The historian Rietschel has proved that the division into " hundari " on the Frisian islands, in Schleswig, Jutland, on the Danish islands and in Southern Sweden was an ancient one, and went back to the time of colonisation. For the long age of this division Rietschel quotes the great number of " hundari " names, each of which is formed by a patronymic family name, ending with the word " kind," which means kinsmen, relations. He rightly says that such a use of family names to describe closed territorial units can only originate from a time when the country became settled by families.

The fact that the Dorians and the related Philistines followed the same arrangements is a further proof that the Norse people already knew this division during the Great Migration. They formed their armies in units of a hundred, which had to be supplied by the individual departmental areas of the country.

It is quite possible that the Atlantis report does in fact describe the organisation of the Nordic circle in the Bronze Age. It is quite unthinkable that these statements, which correspond so closely to the original conditions of land divisions, are just an invention.

However faithful the statements about the organisation of the Atlantean kingdom may be, the statements concerning the number of the soldiers raised in this country seem improbable. According to Plato's assertion there should have been 60,000 " hundari," which were to supply a total of 6,000,000 warriors for the forces. These are figures which by far surpass all that we know about the strength of the armed forces of that time. There must be an error here.

The cause of this error may be explained as follows: When Solon translated the original Egyptian report into Greek, he unfortunately chose the Greek word "stadia " for the words " hind " or " landless." The impression was thereby created that a " landless," or " hind," was of the size of only one square " stadia," about nine acres. As according to the correct statement the Atlantean kingdom was about the size of 3,000 stadia by 2,000, that is 6,000,000

square stadia, there must have been an equal number of
" hinds." Without doubt a " landless-hind " was not one,
but twenty to thirty square stadia. It is possible that the
exaggerated statement about the strength of the Atlantean
forces can be traced back to the Egyptian sources of the
Atlantis report. Ramses III repeatedly asserted that he had
seen " one hundred thousand, or even one million North
people."

### 3.   THE ROYAL ISLAND BASILEIA

When we now turn to the description of the island of
Basileia we must realise that conditions are described here
which are very similar to those still to be found on the
remaining islands of the " sunk " Westlands of Sylt, Fohr
and Amrum.

According to the Atlantis report, the hills along the coast
of Basileia were not very high, and the opening for the canal
through these hills was only about ninety feet deep. Behind
these hills lay a plain of unsurpassed beauty, traversed by
numerous artificial and natural water arteries. The plain
was not much above sea level, because it is said that during
summer the country was watered by the canal.

Because of the lowness of the country the inhabitants of
Basileia were forced to build dikes. We see from the report
that two concentrically arranged ring dikes were built on
Basileia. The statement that these dikes were built by
Poseidon indicates their extreme age. The dikes were
thrown up from the ground, and, as we are told later, were
strengthened from the outside by a wall of posts. Narrow
roads passed through the dikes and on these roads were
erected towers and gates, which can only be described as
sluices.

It sounds somewhat incredible that dikes and sluices
already existed during the Bronze Age. But it is impossible to
dismiss Plato's statements as sheer invention simply because
these installations did not exist in the Mediterranean
countries during ancient times; especially as Homer, as we
shall see, describes these installations independently from
the Atlantis report.

As the land which was protected during the Bronze Age by the dikes is now below sea level, having been destroyed by the sea, dike installations dating from the Bronze Age are no more in existence. Schuchardt, however, has pointed out that similar constructions existed in Northern Germany in the later Stone Age. The " crannogs " in Britain are also circular earth walls, strengthened by a post barrier, and they certainly originated during the Bronze Age.

Both in front and behind the dikes, so it was reported, was a harbour. On the sea coast, at the mouth of the canal which ran from the capital, was a great " export station." According to the report the export station and the bigger harbour were crowded with the ships of merchants who had assembled there from all over the country, and their feverish activity throughout day and night resulted in a tremendous hubbub. There can be no doubt that a brisk movement of ships must have taken place here. The superb position of Basileia at the mouths of the Rivers Weser, Elbe and Eider enabled it to perform the functions later taken over by the towns of Bremen, Hamburg and Lübeck. Here the " gold of the North," the desirable amber, was dug out of the ground at many places and sent to distant lands. Rich deposits of copper and the much-desired pure copper were to be found here. Merchandise from far-away countries, destined for settlements along the Rivers Weser, Elbe and the Baltic coast was unloaded here, especially zinc from Ireland; ships landed quantities of timber required for the " public " installations (dikes and copper extraction) and for private work. In short, one of the most important harbours of the Bronze Age must have been situated at this spot.

In the centre of the island there is said to have been not only a cold but also a warm spring. Cold springs certainly existed on the sunken Westlands and still exist today on the remaining West German islands. A warm spring, however, seems incredible. But the reliability of this ancient statement is vouchsafed by the following fact. German neswpapers reported on September 1st, 1949, that the investigations of the German geologist Heck on the island of Sylt proved that the interior of the island contained radio-active springs with a temperature of 110–130 deg. Fahrenheit. These springs, which are of great importance for medical purposes, are now to be exploited.

Why should warm springs, which have so recently been discovered on Sult, have been impossible on Basileia?

The hill, upon which stood the royal castle, was said to have a diameter of 3,000 feet. Around the hill was built a protective wall, protected in turn by an outer wall of stone. Within this powerful circumvallation stood the castle and the temple of Poseidon.

On July 31st, 1952, this great wall was discovered at the stated spot, six miles from Heligoland towards the mainland. The investigations carried out by a diver and an echograph have shown an astonishing agreement between the Atlantis report and the ruins examined.

The statements concerning the position of Basileia in the North Sea area also correspond with the facts. As we have seen, the distance northwards to the open sea, to the Skagerrak, amounted to two hundred miles. Further north still are the Norwegian mountains, and it was said that the size and beauty of these mountains were unsurpassed. According to the report, there were many settlements, distant rivers, seas and meadows in this mountain country, and the great mountains were covered with the most diverse kinds of trees. The report states that the timber used for public and private work on Basileia was felled in the woods of those mountains.

These statements show that the original report is based on the account of someone with an intimate knowledge of these parts. His descriptions were of course difficult to understand without maps and knowledge of the North, and therefore liable to misunderstandings and wrong explanations. Furthermore, as with the name " Rome," which sometimes means only the capital, at others the whole Roman Empire, the name " Atlantis " denotes both the royal isle and the whole Atlantean kingdom. This has led to several misconceptions. For example, the original report stated that Atlantis, the royal isle, was surrounded by a water ditch; the traditional sources have mistakenly concluded that this ditch surrounded the whole Atlantean kingdom, and on the basis of this misunderstanding Plato calculated that the water ditch must have been a thousand miles long. Similarly the original report said that Atlantis, the royal isle, submerged under the sea. The traditional sources have drawn from this the wrong conclusion, that Atlantis, the whole Atlantean kingdom, sank beneath the sea. This confusion between the royal isle and the whole of the remaining country is already evident in contemporary inscriptions. Some of them say that only the " chief of its towns," or islands, were torn away by the storms, whilst others say that the whole country perished. The Egyptian writers evidently had no idea of the extent of the catastrophic floods in the North Sea area.

In other parts of the Atlantis report misunderstandings easily arose. Plato asserts that Atlantis was " larger," " more extensive " (*meizon*), than Libya and Asia Minor. The Greek word " *meizon* " can mean both " larger in size " and " more powerful." As the size of the Atlantean kingdom is given between two hundred and three hundred miles, whereas Asia Minor is considerably bigger, in this context the word " *meizon* " should be translated not by " larger in size," but by " more powerful," which corresponds much better to the actual facts.

## BASILEIA, THE " HOLY ISLAND "

ATLANTIS-BASILEIA, the royal island of the Atlanteans, is also called " *Nesos hiera*," because it played an outstanding part in the culture and beliefs, as well as in the legal matters, of the Atlantean kingdom.

As related in the Atlantis report, on this island once stood the highest sanctum of the Atlanteans; here the ten kings of the whole kingdom gathered to worship. The most important religious festivals took place here; the highest court of the land had its seat here to pronounce judgments for the whole kingdom.

The name " Heligoland," or Holy Land (*terra sancta*), as the ruin of the sunken royal isle was already called before its resettlement by Christian monks around A.D. 1000, has kept the memory of the important religious meaning of the island until our days. Adam of Bremen reported that this place was sacred to all seamen, particularly pirates, and that no one returned home unpunished who carried off the island any booty, however small.

### 1. A TROJAN CASTLE ON BASILEIA

That Basileia was a " holy " island is shown by the immense buildings for public worship which had been erected there. It is related that in the centre of the island on the sacred place of Poseidon stood the holy pillar of Atlas, and around this pillar were drawn, " as if measured by a compass," five concentric circles, two of earth and three of water. It is said that Poseidon himself erected this building, " at the beginning when there were no ships." It is said that originally it could not be entered by people.

These statements make it probable that the scholar W. Pastor was correct when he says that Plato described as the highest sacred place of the Atlanteans a proper walled castle surrounded by joined rings.

Walled castles, also called Trojan castles, are natural or artificial hills, surrounded by concentric walls or stone circles, which, according to the German scholar E. Krause, represent very old places of sun worship. A great number of Trojan castles are known in all the territories of Indo-Germanic settlement. The legend has often survived that in these castles a woman or girl was kept prisoner. The same is said in the Atlantis report of Cleito, who was kept prisoner by Poseidon on a hill in the centre of the five circles. These legends are based on an ancient sun myth. The imprisoned woman or maiden represents the sun. The concentric circles, which in later times were spiral shaped, symbolise the path which the sun has to follow in order to escape from its imprisonment. The sun is forced through the circles of spirals to return continuously to its starting point. It is probable that this was a primitive, magical method of influencing the sun to remain on its course.

¹ In the whole field of Trojan castles memories have been preserved of special mystical dances, which had as their purpose the magical influencing, or at least representation, of the course of the sun. The Labyrinth dance of Crete or of Delos, the Trojan dance of the Romans, the British dances in the Trojan castle of Wisby and Goathland have all been handed down to us in literature or custom. We shall hear that on Basileia also a similar " divine dance " was danced.

The concentric form of circles, as described in the Atlantis report, is according to the investigations of Krause and Schwantes the oldest form, out of which later grew the spiral-shaped structures. Krause thinks that the concentric structures are mostly buildings from the early Stone Age. Schwantes mentions symbolic decorations on mystical stones, bronzes and idols dating from the later Bronze Age or early Stone Age; their concentric, or spiral-shaped, sun symbols show an uncanny similarity with those structures, being completely similar in every detail. One of the most famous of the stone circles still in existence today is the great stone structure at Stonehenge in Wiltshire.

As Krause and Pastor have shown, the representation of the course of the sun by circles of different sizes can only have originated in the North, because only there does the sun's course apparently describe circles varying greatly in size. Pastor noticed that the artificial circles on Atlantis were of quite different sizes. As he believes these artificial rings to be imitations of the winter and summer courses of the sun, he came to the conclusion that the model for the Trojan castle on Atlantis originated in Northern Europe. Like many of his contemporaries, Pastor hoped to find Atlantis in the Azores, and he asserted that the circles were a clear proof that Teutonic North Europe must have been the giver, while Atlantis was the receiver. Northern Europe was therefore not a cultural province of Atlantis, but on the contrary Atlantis was a cultural province of Northern Europe.

Had he known that Atlantis was situated in Northern Europe, and not near the Azores, he would have had fresh and remarkable proof for his theory that the Trojan castles originated in Northern Europe. The striking similarity, if not complete exactness, of numerous Trojan castles in the whole of the Indo-Germanic settlement areas has often led to the assumption that these structures could ultimately be traced back to one original pattern.

Where are we to find this prototype of all Trojan castles? That it has to be found in the Nordic areas has been convincingly shown by Krause and Pastor. Was it perhaps the structure on Atlantis? The following facts seem to confirm this view. According to the Atlantis report, this structure was built " at the beginning when man first walked on this earth and when there were no ships." It was built by Poseidon himself, called by Homer the oldest and noblest of all gods. The structure on Basileia was, according to the stated measurements, the biggest, and because of its embellishment with amber by far the most striking. It stood upon the island, called the " holy island " in the Atlantis report, which asserts that it was the cultural centre of the North.

This structure on Basileia was connected with a "world pillar cult" which could certainly claim a very old age. All these statements make us believe that we have to look for the "prototype" in the structure of Atlantis-Basileia, if the Trojan castles can be traced back at all to a definite "prototype."

It does not really matter what we think the answer to this problem may be; what is certain is that the whole story about the Trojan castle on Basileia cannot be a fairy-tale invented by Solon or Plato. The description in the report must be based on a Trojan castle which did in fact once exist.

## 2.   THE " WORLD PILLAR CULT " ON BASILEIA

On the basis of his detailed investigation into Trojan castles Krause came to the conclusion that these structures must have originally been connected with the cult of a "world axis god," like Atlas, because the centre of the concentric circles representing the course of the sun was believed to have been the world axis, or world pillar carrying the heaven. Krause was unable to substantiate this feasible assumption by any facts. Had he known the Atlantis report, however, and known that it described very ancient customs of the North, then he would have found substantial proof for his theory.

The Atlantis report emphatically states that on Atlantis a holy pillar stood in the centre of the concentric circles; order and unity amongst themselves were supported by the rules of Poseidon, as handed down by the law and the inscriptions engraved by the ancient fathers on a pillar made of amber. This pillar stood in the centre of the island on the sanctuary of Poseidon. There the kings gathered every five or six years, in order not to favour either the even or uneven number, and they consulted each other about their common affairs; they investigated whether any of them was guilty of a trespass and gave judgment accordingly. But when they resolved to hold a court of law they made the following pledge to each other: in the holy area of Poseidon there grazed some bulls. " The Ten " organised a hunt without weapons, except sticks, and prayed to their god that they should catch the bull chosen by their god. The captured bull was sacrificed at the same height as the inscription. On the pillar there was inscribed in addition to the law the words of an oath invoking curses upon the disobedient. After the lawful sacrifice they offered all the limbs of the bull to the god; as a dedication they poured the blood into a basin which was ready for this purpose, and the rest they threw into the fire, after having cleansed the pillar. They then drank from golden drinking mugs out of the basin and swore that they would rule according to the laws on the pillar, and mete out punishment if one of them was guilty of an offence. So far as the future was concerned, no one would intentionally be guilty of an offence against the law, nor would he rule against the law, nor obey a ruler who did not follow the laws of his own father.

The pillar thus described, which stood in the centre of the sanctuary and therefore of the Trojan castle of Atlantis, was without doubt a " world column." The report that the sacrificed animal was killed high up on the pillar shows that the pillar had extended arms at its top, upon which a bull could stand. The shape of this pillar is known to us from a representation of a " world pillar " on a Philistine basin dating from the time around 1160 B.C.

The Nordic idea of the " universe, or Heaven's pillar " holding up the sky, was known in the South quite early. In the inscription of Thutmose III (around 1500 B.C.) we learn of the pillars of heaven in the North. Ramses II (1292–1232) asserted that his fame and power extended from the southern negro lands to the marshlands at the borders of darkness, where stood the four pillars of heaven. In a witchcraft book dating to the age of Ramses III mention is made of the " carrying gods, which live in the darkness, in the far North." In the Book of Hiob also mention is made of the " columns of heaven," at the ends of the seas where light and darkness separate.

The Greeks called these pillars " Pillars of Atlas." The Greek myth maintains that this name was given to the " world pillars," because Atlas, the king who gave the island

Irminsul = World Pillar:

(1) Philistine bowl from 1160 B.C.;　　(2) Drawing from the *Externstein*.

Atlantis its name, was the first to calculate the movements of the stars. The legend was thereby created that Atlas was carrying the columns of heaven. Homer knew Atlas only as someone who supports the immense pillars which bear both heaven and earth. Hesiod has told us where Atlas carries the pillars of heaven: at the ends of the earth, at the dwellings of night, where day and night are near to each other and converse with each other.

When the ancients talked of " borders of darkness," or " dwellings of the night," then they always meant the far North, as mentioned before. The pillars of heaven are therefore also called " *stele boreios* "—" Pillars of the North." The legend says later that Atlas gave the pillars of heaven to Hercules to bear, and for this reason these pillars of the North, or pillars of Atlas, were later called " Pillars of Hercules." After the sixth or fifth century B.C., when the North gradually disappeared from the horizon of the Mediterranean peoples, the Straits of Gibraltar became known as " Pillars of Hercules." There seems to be little doubt that the original Pillars of Hercules in the North were situated in the land of amber, on Basileia.

Tacitus also mentions these " Pillars of Hercules " in the North Sea. He said that they " remained until the present day." Drusus Germanicus attempted to investigate them, " but the sea did not allow this."

Seneca speaks of these pillars in a description of a North Sea voyage. There they are called " turning-points of things," they were " situated in the sea of mud," at the far

borders of the world, " in the holy waters, near the seat of
the gods."

Sophocles mentioned the pillars of heaven in the land
of the Hyperboreai, at the farthest corner of the world, at the
springs of night, the resting place of the sun, the " changing
of the stars." There can be no doubt that these " pillars of
heaven," "Pillars of Hercules," must have described the
holy pillar of the universe in the centre of the sanctuary of
the North, in the temple of Atlantis-Basileia. No wonder
that Tacitus said of this pillar that it remained in existence
until his own times.

We have already ascertained that Basileia must have
appeared again after the sea regression of the Iron Age and
it might also have been settled anew between the fourth and
first century B.C.

From this concept of the world pillar there developed later
among the Teutons concepts of the world navel and the
world tree and the belief that the world would collapse if
these were torn out. Jung believes that the Roland pillars
must be regarded as remains of the cult of world pillars.
This ancient concept of the world pillar in the Nordic area
has remained until the Christian era. The unique importance of the pillar cult of the North people, or Philistines, is
also shown by the Old Testament name for Atlantis-Basileia.
The ancient country of the Philistines is called " ai Caphtor,"
which means island of pillars (Jeremiah xlvii. 4), and the
Philistines themselves are called " Caphtorites," meaning
" people of pillars." It is mentioned repeatedly in the Old
Testament that the Philistines worshipped pillars in their
country.

The world pillar must have been of enormous dimensions.
Rudolf of Fulda (A.D. 850) reported that it took three days
to destroy the world pillar. In the German Emperor
Chronicle it is related that the Romans had slain Julius
Cæsar but that they had buried him on a world pillar.
Elsewhere in the Chronicle Simon the Conjurer stood on a
world pillar in order to be seen by as many people as
possible. The statement of the Atlantis report concerning
the wonderful decoration of the world pillar is confirmed by a

chronicle dating from the year A.D. 772 which says that the pillar was decorated with artistic ornaments and decorations. The custom reported in the Atlantis legend that sacrificial blood was poured over the world pillar remained in existence until the time of the Christian conversion. It is not improbable that the world pillar on Atlantis was the " prototype " of all other world pillars. Reminders as to the form and cult of this pillar have been kept alive through many thousands of years.

### 3.   THE RITUAL OF THE BULL SACRIFICE ON BASILEIA

We learn from the Atlantis report that inseparably connected with the world pillar cult was a ceremonial bull sacrifice. It was said that in the area of the holy temple around the world pillar were kept freely grazing bulls. As already mentioned the ten kings had to catch one of these bulls to be sacrificed to their god, " without iron, only with sticks and rope." The bull to be sacrificed was taken to the holy world pillar, and slaughtered there so that its blood poured over the pillar. The bull was then cut up according to precise regulations and finally delivered to the holy fire, with the exception of ten drops of blood, which were sprinkled into a holy basin.

The description of the bull sacrifice shows that we are concerned here with a very ancient cult. This is proved by the fact that when the bull was caught only the most ancient and primitive weapons of man, such as sticks and rope, were used, and not contemporary weapons. The formality that one king " alone " could catch the bull is an indication that the cult dated from a time when the tribal chiefs, who originally were always the highest sacrifice priests, caught a wild bull with stick and rope for the holy sacrifice. It is usually assumed that this was the original purpose of the animal capture. Animals were caught for ceremonial sacrifices long before they were caught for the purpose of rearing.

This form of religious worship dates to a cultural phase long before that mentioned in the Atlantis report. This report describes the cultural stage of the peasant and cattle-breeder. According to all indications the bull sacrifice dates back to the stage of the hunter. The bull sacrifice seems to have been a rather rare and exclusive festival in the age of Atlantis. It only took place every five or six years and was reserved solely for " the Ten." Hofler's remark about the astonishing tenacity by which these forms of civilisation lasted for thousands of years could also be applied to this festival. Dating from the civilisation of the hunter, surviving the thousands of years of the Stone Age, it towered over the peasant civilisation of the Bronze Age like a megalith grave in our time.

Hauer was the first to recognise in this bull sacrifice on Atlantis the ancient Indo-Germanic bull cult. This cult belongs inseparably to the world pillar cult, because wherever the latter cult has survived into later ages, the world pillar was rubbed with sacrificial blood as on Atlantis. Jung says that it was believed that the rubbing of the world support contributed towards the keeping up of the world. This bull sacrifice was still customary in later times in the cults of the North people, as for instance the Cymbrians and Teutons.

### 4. THE FIRE CULT

Like the world pillar cult, the fire cult also played an important part in the holy festival on Basileia. We are told that, as soon as darkness came and the fire of sacrifice was extinguished, " the Ten " put on blue garments of great beauty. They sat by the glow of the sacrificial oath fire and extinguished all other fires around the sanctuary. It was said earlier that the remains of the bull were thrown into the fire and that its blood, which " the Ten " drank from golden cups, was sprinkled into the fire of sacrifice.

These statements evidently describe the fire cult as it was customary with all Indo-Germanic peoples. Through the great sacrifices which were thrown into the fire it was apparently believed that new strength would be added to the diminishing warmth of the sun. The extinguishing of the old fires, the solemn kindling of a new fire, or the relighting of the ancient holy fire with ample sacrificial gifts, were an important part of the ancient Indo-Germanic fire cult. Among the Teutons, in whose connection Cæsar mentions the fire cult, the holy fire was called " *hnot-fiur*," which derives from " *niuwan, hniotan*," which means " rubbing." In many German country districts the custom long remained to make the new holy fire by rubbing pieces of wood. Often only twins were allowed to carry out this procedure. In the Rig-veda, an ancient Indian writing of 1100–1000 B.C., it is reported that the holy function of fire rubbing must be carried out by the godlike twins Acvins, who are very like the ancient Teutonic twins Alcis.

On the picture stone of Kivik, one of the oldest documents of ancient Teutonic religion, dating back to 1500 B.C., the holy procedure of fire rubbing is represented by two men who are possibly twins. On Atlantis also twins seem to have played an important rôle. Poseidon is said to have begotten five pairs of twins with Cleito, and he is said to have divided his kingdom amongst the ten twins. According to the Atlantis report, " the Ten " are direct descendants of these twins. As they arranged " by themselves " the world pillar, bull sacrifice, new-fire festival, we can assume that these twin kings also carried out the important kindling of the new fire. On the stone of Kivik the holy ritual of the new kindling is accompanied by lute music. This was possibly also the case on Atlantis, although it was not mentioned in the report. The fact that all other fires around the sanctuary had to be extinguished during this festival and only the new fire could remain alight is also known from a later period in the Indo-Germanic area.

### 5. THE BLUE MANTLE OF THE KING

In the description of the highest festival of the Atlanteans the blue coat, or mantle, is mentioned. It was worn by each of the ten kings during the great festival and was said to have been exceptionally beautiful. These blue coats were only worn for a short time at the height of the festival, and afterwards these special garments were kept in the temple beside the golden table of laws.

It is a strange coincidence that just such a royal blue mantle, belonging, however, to a much later time, the third century A.D., was found during excavations on the Thorsberger Moor in Schleswig-Holstein. Schlabow, who examined it closely, and also reconstructed it, confirmed that the " technical miracle " of this mantle lies not so much in its length (at least seven feet), but more in its manufacture; two different kinds of weaving were used and could only have been performed by a highly developed weaving apparatus. Schlabow was able to prove that this highly developed weaver's loom must have already been used during the Bronze Age, three thousand five hundred years before. The colour of the mantle was not, as originally believed, green, but a brilliant blue. Infra-red photographs have shown that the yarn material for tying around the body did not consist of a single tone of blue but graduated shades of dark, medium and light.

As the weaver's loom which was used for the manufacture of these impressive garments could be traced back as far as the Bronze Age, we can safely assume that the blue mantles of the kings on Atlantis were very like the one found in Thorsberg, as far as cut and colour are concerned. On the picture stones of Kivik the men wear long coats, exactly as has been reported of the Atlantean kings during the great sacrifice.

### 6. THE HOLY VESSEL

A holy vessel played an important part during the great festival. It stood in the centre of " the Ten " during the festivities, and the bull's blood which flowed down the world pillar was caught in it. Out of it into golden cups was ladled the holy drink, which was probably meant to connect " the Ten " with their god and with each other.

There can be no doubt that such a sacrificial basin played a special rôle in the Nordic area. Several of them have been found in Teutonic territories, and some are beautifully decorated and can be driven on wheels. It is reported that the Cymbrians offered the Roman emperor Augustus their holy sacrificial basin when they sent a deputation to Rome in exchange for a naval visit by Tiberius in A.D. 500. The Philistines also possessed such holy basins at the time of the destruction of Atlantis. On Cyprus, for example, a vessel was found in Philistine graves dating to 1200 B.C. which is remarkably similar to the Nordic, Bronze Age basins.

On the picture stones of Kivik a great basin is in the centre of the sacrificers. Figures robed in long garments are approaching the holy basin from both sides, to drink from it the holy drink. Golden sacrifice cups, as used by " the Ten " for drinking of bull's blood, have been found in the Nordic area in great numbers. Especially worth mentioning in this connection are two golden drinking mugs with bull's heads from the island of Zealand, which were found on a hill which had originally been three terraces and evidently was once a Trojan castle.

## 7. THE STATUE OF POSEIDON

The report relates of the statue of Poseidon in the sanctuary on Basileia: They erected in the temple pictures of a god in gold, the god standing on a cart drawn by six winged horses of such size that the god's head touched the ceiling.

The statements concerning the size, number and making of the golden pictures are without doubt exaggerated. It is possible that the Egyptian priests decorated the original accounts of the images in the Nordic temples with their own symbols. There were in Egypt enormous, larger-than-life-sized images of gods, covered with gold plate and embellished with precious stones. We cannot, however, dismiss the whole description on account of these exaggerations, as we have, in the pictures from the Kivik grave, representations of the god in pictures.

On a stone of the Kivik grave a god is represented standing on a carriage guiding a team of horses. To the left of the team is a large dolphin beside which are two idle horses. Below these are eight statues draped in long garments.

This stone picture on Kivik probably presents in the concise form of the rock pictures of the Stone Age the same group of statues which is described in the Atlantis report. The gravestone of Kivik confirms that the god's picture mentioned in the report already existed three hundred years before the sinking of Atlantis.

How can this representation of Poseidon be explained? It is generally agreed that the goddess represented on the Kivik stone must be interpreted as a sun deity. A god drives the sun carriage, to which are harnessed the sun horses, over the heavens. In ancient times it was believed that the sun, which sets in the sea at night, when the sun horses are free, is drawn by dolphins through the underworld to its starting point in the East. The sun horses, therefore, represent the day course and the dolphins the night course of the sun. This ancient belief is shown on the Kivik stone by the dolphin beside the horses, which are free during the night. The female figures pictured in the lowest group of the stone are evidently the nymphs which are mentioned in the Atlantis report as accompanying the sun god.

Many Nordic gods have female attendants. Atlas, for example, is said to have been accompanied by the Hesperides, Helios by the Heliades. In later times the Valkyrie belonged to Wotan, the Idis to Donat and the Nymphs to Balder. In Northern Friesland legend tells of women who come from the sea and disappear there, of sea maidens who live in a glass palace at the bottom of the sea, who change into swans and infatuate young fishermen, or sing songs of farewell to the drowned. The Nereids, or sea nymphs, were evidently such sea maidens, and appear therefore in the retinue of Poseidon.

The tomb of Kivik proves that all the things related in the Atlantis report really existed in the religion of the North: the lighting of the new fire, a holy vessel, a supreme god who stood guiding the sun horses on a carriage surrounded by nymphs and Nereids. There is nothing to disprove the belief that the pictures in the tomb of Kivik represent a festival on Atlantis-Basileia. Perhaps the great person buried in the enormous tomb of Kivik belonged to those kings who gathered every five or six years at the great law-giving assembly on Basileia.

The Old Testament also tells of the great " moulded " statues of the god of the Philistines. It is reported there that in their temples at Gaza and Asdod was a statue of their highest god in human form. This god is described with the Semitic word " *Dagon*," which means " fish god." There can be no doubt that the " fish god " of the Philistines was the same as the god with the fish once worshipped by their ancestors on Atlantis-Basileia and which has been preserved for us on the tombstone of Kivik. The identity between Dagon and Poseidon has been ascertained by Hitzig, the investigator of the history of the Philistines, after detailed research.

### 8.  THE TEMPLE OF POSEIDON ON BASILEIA

According to the statements of the Atlantis report, the temple of Poseidon on Basileia had a barbaric appearance. This description may have been an indication that it looked different from an Egyptian or Greek temple. The temple is said to have been five hundred feet long and two hundred and fifty feet wide. Gold, silver and amber covered to an excessive degree the exterior and interior of the sanctuary. These statements sound so incredible that one is inclined to dismiss them as fairy-tales. There are, however, reports of temples and sanctuaries from ancient Teutonic sources which sound no less fantastic. It was said, for instance, of the temple of Fosites that it was of a superb size and simply covered with gold and precious jewels. According to the tradition of Edda, Glitnir, the amber temple of Fosites, is said to have had walls, posts and pillars made of red gold, and a roof of silver. " Gimle," the precious-stone hall, was covered with gold, according to Edda. The famous temple of Thor in Uppsala is said to have had a roof of gold, walls covered with gold and precious jewels, and a golden curtain. The glass tower, or glass hill, of Teutonic legend, which dates back at least to 2000 B.C., is said to have been as big as a hill and to have had a layer of copper, silver and one of gold. We cannot dismiss the statement of the Atlantis report as an illusion or fairy-tale, as at least it is based on an ancient Teutonic myth which is known to the present day.

It is important to realise that according to the Atlantis

report the whole of the temple of Poseidon on Basileia was covered with orichalc, or amber. Floors, walls, pillars and ceilings glittered with this " Nordic " gold, which, as we know, was found in many parts of Basileia. That this description is very near the truth can be seen from the following observations; we shall see that Homer has described in detail the royal isle of Atlantis. He used a source independent of the Atlantis report and he says that " like the rays of the sun and the glimmer of the moon does the home of Alkinoos glitter." It is obvious that he is describing a hall made of amber. We have already heard that the many legends in the Nordic area which tell of a " glass tower," or a " glass castle," are probably reminders of the amber temple on Basileia. It is not surprising that the ancient legends described this temple as a house of the dead, or as a " home for the departed dead." According to the investigations of Professor Huth, the sun, fertility and death cults formed an entity in the megalithic age from which this temple originates. It has therefore always been a sanctuary for these cults, and so became a " house of the dead " in Nordic legend. The ancient Frisian legend says that at the bottom of the sea near Heligoland there is a house of the dead with walls of glass and a crystal roof where sea nymphs sing their funeral hymns. The British history of Nennius, dating back to the ninth century A.D., relates that beyond the sea there is an island upon which stands a high glass tower and which is also the Isle of the Blessed.

We repeatedly find in ancient legends the statement that the world tree stands on the top of the glass hill. This seems to have been the case on Basileia. Other legends strangely relate that the glass hill was surrounded by three water rings, as was the case with the highest sanctuary on Basileia. All these statements and traditional sources make it seem possible that the amber temple on Basileia and the glass hill, or glass tower, of the legend are connected with each other. Either the legends of the glass tower contain a reminder of the chief sanctuary of the North, or the latter obeyed the ancient mythical conceptions which are the basis of the glass tower legend. It is irrelevant in this context which theory we favour, but we can safely imagine that the temple of Atlantis looked like the glass tower, or hill, of the ancient Teutonic legend. Huth has shown that the glass tower probably consisted of three floors, on the top of which could be found the world tree. These structures were imitations of the three-storey world hill, a symbol which is characteristic of the megalithic circle of civilisation. There seems little doubt that the religious structures on Basileia were already erected in the megalithic age. The room in which Cleito gave birth to the first twin kings was still shown in the sanctuary at the time of the sinking of Atlantis. Then the sanctuary was regarded as a very ancient structure.

It is possible that in the sanctuary on Basileia a golden apple was kept and worshipped. Some ancient Teutonic legends report that on top of the glass tower sat a royal daughter who carried a golden apple in her hand. Homer mentions the wonderful apple orchard on this royal isle. In the ancient Greek myth it is reported that the Hesperides gave apples of immortality. An ancient Greek vase picture shows Atlas handing Hercules the golden apple. According to ancient Teutonic sources, the apples of Idun are kept in Asgard, in front of which is situated the *Glasir*, or amber forest. According to Celtic legend, the glass island is called *Avalun*, which means " apple island." Pliny asserts that Pytheas called the island Basileia in the North Sea *Abalus*, which also means " apple island." The English chronicler William of Malmesbury calls the glass island *Insula Avalloniæ*, which he himself translated as " apple island." He also reports that the first founder of the glass tower, Glastening, is said to have planted a wonderful orchard of apples which give immortality. According to ancient Celtic legends King Arthur was taken to the glass island of Avalun to rule in those fields of the blessed until his return.

We do not find, however, any mention in the Atlantis report of the golden apples. We learn, though, from ancient Greek sources that Atlas kept the golden apple on an island in the Northern Ocean, in the neighbourhood of the Hyperboreoi. Only Atlantis-Basileia can be meant by this island of Atlas in the Northern Ocean. In this case a golden apple must have played a rôle in the cult, which, although the Atlantis report is silent about it, is well documented by the above-quoted traditional sources.

## 9. SPORT AND GAMES ON BASILEIA

The Atlantis report also mentions places of sport, competitions and chariot races. We learn that swimming pools and wash-houses were built by Poseidon near the springs on the royal hill. There were also training places for gymnastic purposes for men and tracks for chariot races.

These statements sound rather fanciful, but immense places of contests have been found in the Nordic area dating back to the Bronze Age. We have, moreover, a witness for these statements—Homer, who confirms them in all details, and even takes us to an athletic contest on the sports grounds of Basileia.

Among the racecourses of the Bronze Age still in existence today must be counted the stone circle of Stonehenge which must have been erected by men of the Atlantean culture many centuries before the Atlantis report was written. The racecourse at Stonehenge, in its original, immense dimensions, cannot be an imitation of a Greek stadium.

We shall hear later about the places of contests and competitions on Basileia, as described by Homer. These carriage races were originally ceremonies connected with the death cult; Professor Huth believes this was so in Germany and Ireland, at least, and both countries must have belonged to the Atlantean sphere of influence during the Bronze Age. All these statements suggest that the Norse people must have reached a high state of physical fitness during the Bronze Age. When they were driven from their homes by the catastrophes of the thirteenth century B.C. and settled in Greece, they found in the subsequently famous region of Olympia (destroyed in the battles around 1200 B.C.) only secular settlements. In their place the new masters built a great religious centre with a temple of Apollo similar to the Poseidon temple on Atlantis, and a temple of Cronos, who, according to legend, was a brother of Atlas and a king of the

Atlanteans. As on Atlantis, the famous places of contest of
Olympia were built near the temple. These structures were
built, according to Greek myths, by " men of the golden
race," which means the Atlanteans. It was said of the holy
tree in Olympia, from which a laurel wreath was cut with a
golden knife for the victor of the various competitions, that it
was brought by Hercules from the Northlands to Olympia.
On the late geometric vases made by descendants of the
North people who invaded Greece around 1200 B.C., racing
chariots and competitions were often painted, which clearly
shows the fighting spirit brought to the South by the North
people from their athletics arenas. There is a strong connection between the many sports and contest places of Atlantis-
Basileia and those of Olympia. The gallant, fighting spirit
which was cultivated in the Olympiads and which has been
preserved until our times had its birthplace not in Olympia,
but on Basileia, where it was fostered and encouraged many
centuries before the construction of the Olympic courses.

Homer knew nothing of Olympia and the Olympic games,
but he knew of Atlantis-Basileia and its racecourses, and he
celebrated in immortal verses the gallant fighting spirit
which prevailed.

# CONCLUSIONS

THE investigation of the various statements of the Atlantis report have shown that many of them correspond to historical, geographical and cultural facts.

The story of the Atlantis report, that at the time when copper and zinc were used almost exclusively although the first iron was known, i.e. the thirteenth century B.C., a terrible climatic catastrophe afflicted the world, and in the whirl of great heat and drought, earthquakes and floods, a very favourable climatic period came to an end, is in agreement with the latest results of climatic research. Also corresponding to historical facts is the statement that during that time a migration of the largest dimensions took place through Europe and Asia Minor as far as Egypt; it overran many countries, destroyed the countries in South-Eastern Europe and came to a standstill only at the Egyptian border.

Archæological excavations have shown that the town of Athens, as maintained by the Atlantis report, defended herself successfully and saved her freedom. The statements of the Atlantis report, that the main force of this wave came from the islands and coastlands on the North Sea, and that the Tyrrhenians and Libyans were in alliance with them, is confirmed by many contemporary inscriptions and documents. These documents also confirm that numerous islands, including the island with a royal town, were torn away and destroyed. The statements that immediately before the

Fallen Northern warrior with horn helmet.

Libyan and Northern prisoners being led away.

Northern rock drawing from Vadebacka, West Gotland. The figure on the right wears a reed crown.

royal isle Basileia was a rock island of red, white and black stone; that the hill on which stood the royal castle was six miles distant from the rock island; and that amber-orichalc was found in many places in the ground whilst copper was found in pure form, also correspond to the known facts. Furthermore, the statement that this area of Basileia was changed after the catastrophe into an impassable sea of mud, thereby blocking the passage to the outer sea, is also without doubt correct. The statements of the Atlantis report concerning the size of the Atlantean kingdom, its organisation and army formation can most likely be confirmed by the research which has so far been carried out in this field. Similarly the statements about religious beliefs in the home island of the Atlanteans seem to contain a large measure of truth. The rock pictures in the tomb of Kivik show that during the Bronze Age in the North a god was indeed worshipped, who was pictured standing on a chariot, accompanied by dolphins and sea nymphs, exactly as told in the Atlantis report. The statements about the worshipping of the world pillar, the bull sacrifice and the embellishment of the temple with amber also appear to be authentic. They are confirmed in later times by the beliefs of the Norse people, by legend and tradition.

Amongst these statements there are some which must be attributed to only one expert eye-witness. The authority who told of the red, white and black colour of the rock island, who gave the correct distance of the castle hill to the mainland, who knew of copper and amber deposits on Basileia and many other details, must have been a native of the country. The precise knowledge of the rare and exclusive ceremony of the bull sacrifice gives support to the assumption that this authority must be found amongst the " gathering of the Ten."

Ramses III points out in his inscriptions that amongst the captured North people, of whom Ramses II said there were more than a hundred thousand, there must have been " the Ten " who were the leaders, or kings, of the North people. The great relief which describes the capture of the North people shows how Ramses III himself leads the princes of the

North people away in chains, how he interrogates the captured and how their statements were taken down by many writers. Evidently the detailed knowledge about the Northland and its fate, given not only by contemporary inscriptions but also in the Atlantis report, had been handed down through these captured warriors in Egypt. The Atlantis report confirms this assumption when it says that the original report, quoted by the priests in Sais, was translated from the Atlantean language into Egyptian, and can be traced back to direct statements of the Atlanteans. This report is supported by contemporary inscriptions, because it contains several words which can only be explained, not from Egyptian, but from Indo-Germanic language sources. The word " *nwts*," for example, translated by Breasted, the great American Egyptologist, as " unquiet," and by Grapow as " trembling," cannot be explained in Egyptian and originates from the Indo-Germanic vocabulary. Various translation errors, such as orichalc for amber, " year " instead of " month," show that the original report was not written in Egyptian but must have been translated. We can safely assume that the original report can be traced back to the statements of captured North warriors.

These statements were then kept in the archives of the Egyptian kings, which had existed at least since Thutmose III (around 1500 B.C.), or were chiselled on the walls and pillars of the temple in Sais and Medinet Habu which was erected by Ramses III in thanksgiving for the victory over the North people. When afterwards the priests in Sais were charged by Psamtik I and his successor with the collection and arranging of the ancient documents and inscriptions, these were taken out again and looked into. It is possible that the ancient tales from the time of Ramses III were already embellished and enlarged by Egyptian actions in Sais. Afterwards Solon heard in Sais the old story of the resistance of the Athenians against the Atlanteans, had the report of the Egyptian priests translated into Greek and changed it into a poem. Misunderstandings and wrong translations, embellishments and other changes have crept into the Atlantis report during the course of time.

The main authority for the original report may have been one of " the Ten " captured by Ramses III. On the basis of his exact knowledge, especially of the area around Basileia, it may be assumed that he was the king or prince who himself had a castle on Basileia, and was therefore able to describe the many details so closely and correctly.

## 2. ATTEMPTS UP TO THE PRESENT TO FIX THE DATES AND SITE OF ATLANTIS

The acceptance of the Atlantis report in its original form as a reçord of historical events in the thirteenth century B.C., and of the island Basileia, which it mentions in detail, as identical with the island Basileia mentioned by Pytheas, makes invalid all attempts which have been made so far to date and locate Atlantis.

Of the countless theories which have been put forward about the time of the sinking as well as the position of Atlantis, the following have been received with particular emphasis:

I. Atlantis is identical with Tartessos;
II. Atlantis was destroyed in the neighbourhood of the Azores;
II. Atlantis was situated in the Sahara;
IV. Atlantis is identical with Crete.

I. Adolf Schulten has attempted in numerous writings to prove that Atlantis was identical with Tartessos, the Tarshish of the Bible. Since 1922 he has published a number of works about the commercial centre of Tartessos, situated at the mouth of the River Guadalquivir. According to Schulten, Tartessos was founded in the eleventh century B.C. and is first mentioned by the prophet Isaiah in 740 B.C. and after this in many writings of antiquity. Schulten maintains that it was destroyed by the Carthaginians around 500 B.C. " out of commercial envy." All mention of Tartessos after 500 B.C. is believed by Schulten to be confusion between this town and Gades (now Cadiz), or historically valueless quotations from older sources.

Schulten's argument for identifying Tartessos with Atlantis is based on the statement in the report that Gadeiros, the twin brother of Atlas, received the larger part of the Atlantean kingdom, from the Pillars of Hercules to the district now called Gadeiric. Schulten sees in this sentence undeniable proof for the location of Atlantis in Southern Spain. He adduces a number of similarities between his construction of the conditions of Tartessos, which incidentally he never found, and Atlantis, and he tries in this way to strengthen his theory. The sinking of Atlantis, which is often repeated in the Atlantis report, is understood by Schulten to be a " poetical formulation of the fact that Tartessos was destroyed by the Carthaginians for reasons of commercial envy." Everything that contradicts his views is said to be " in the clouds," or is dismissed as pure fantasy. In this class are all the statements about the climatic catastrophes of that age, the report of the migration of the Atlanteans through Europe and Asia Minor to Egypt, the story of Athens' deliverance, and many others.

Schulten has found enthusiastic followers for his theories. Jesson wrote: " Schulten's theory about Atlantis-Tartessos is an ideal solution." Henning also has supported this solution in many publications.

The following can be said against Schulten's theories:

(1) Schulten completely overlooks the repeated statement of Plato, that the Atlantis report was brought by Solon from Egypt to Greece. As we have shown, this statement corresponds with the facts and is confirmed by Proclos, Plutarch and other writers of antiquity. Solon was in Egypt around 570 B.C. At that time he disclosed that Basileia had been destroyed a long time previously by a terrible flood, which changed the area into an impassable sea of mud. According to Schulten's own statements, Tartessos was destroyed by the Carthaginians around 500 B.C. Solon could not know of this destruction of Tartessos, as it happened many decades after his death, and his story of the sinking of Atlantis could not possibly describe the destruction of Tartessos. Through the alleged destruction of Tartessos by the Carthaginians the area in which Tartessos was situated was not changed into a

sea of mud, the path to the outer sea was not blocked, nor did the destruction of Tartessos cause a great migration through Europe and Asia Minor.

(2) Schulten overlooks the fact that in the Atlantis report it is by no means stated that Atlantis, the sovereignty of Poseidon's eldest son Atlas, was situated near Gadeiros, but near the Gadeiric country, the sovereignty of Gadeiros. This statement is therefore not "infallible proof," but, on the contrary, a clear proof against Schulten's theory, because according to the Atlantis report Atlantis and the Gadeiric land are two different areas, and one could not have been situated where the other was. Furthermore, to make Gadeiros synonymous with Gades is very questionable, as the latter was founded a hundred years after the sinking of Atlantis.

(3) The stories in the Atlantis report about the sinking of Atlantis, the march of the Atlanteans through Europe and Asia Minor to Egypt, the deliverance and heroic struggle of Athens, the great natural catastrophes of that age, etc., are not "figments of the imagination," as maintained by Schulten, or "myths," but reports of historical facts which actually happened in the time of the advent of iron.

(4) It is said of Atlantis in the report that it comprised the islands and parts of the mainland in the North. Tartessos, however, was not situated in the north, but west of Egypt and Greece.

(5) In Plato's time Tartessos was not destroyed, as asserted by Schulten. It is still mentioned after 500 B.C. in the writings of the Old Testament, and in many other Greek and Roman writings long after Plato. It is not good enough to dismiss all these later mentions of Tartessos as misunderstandings or anachronisms.

(6) According to Schulten, Tartessos was founded around 1100 B.C. by the Tyrians from Asia Minor. This could not have been the royal town of the Atlanteans because they were destroyed a hundred years before this time, as is shown by the contemporary inscriptions in Medinet Habu.

(7) As has been proved already, the Atlanteans are not identical with the Tyrians, or Etruscans, but with the North

and Sea peoples of the contemporary Egyptian inscriptions; the Etruscans did not move after the destruction of their islands, through Europe and Asia Minor to Egypt, but this was done by the North Sea peoples, or Atlanteans.

II. The second theory, which has often been expressed of late, asserts that Atlantis is submerged near the Azores at a depth of more than ten thousand feet. This assertion was first expressed by the Jesuit Athanasius Kircher in 1665. In 1784 the Frenchman Cadet elaborated on this view and regarded the islands of the Azores and Canaries as remains of Atlantis. This idea has been enthusiastically taken up by the American Donelly and is championed in many writings by the Englishman Egerton Sykes. The assumption that Atlantis was situated near the Azores where it is submerged at a depth of more than ten thousand feet is from a geological and oceanographic standpoint an absolute impossibility. The Swedish oceanographer Petterson said that this theory is, geophysically speaking, a corpse which can never be brought back to life. The ocean territory around the Azores has been throughly investigated during years of research by the American M. Eving. Countless tests of the sea bed have shown that those areas must have been covered by the sea for at least twenty million years, and have certainly never emerged above sea level since men inhabited this earth. Geological investigations of the Azores by the German Hartung have shown that the sea level around the Azores has changed by not more than a few yards since the last Ice Age. On the sea coast of the Azores today there are countless erratic stone blocks of Arctic or Nordic origin which do not exist on the Azores proper. These stone blocks were deposited in the last Ice Age by icebergs which stranded near the coast and melted there. As they lie on the sea coast nowadays they are an infallible proof that the sea level near the Azores has hardly changed in the last twenty thousand years. The sea level certainly did not rise by ten thousand feet during the Bronze Age, the period covered by the Atlantis report.

For these reasons the theory that Atlantis was situated near the Azores must be discarded. The same applies to the belief that during the Bronze Age a mighty empire with a large population existed near the Azores, and that from there a gigantic population movement took place during the time of the first iron, penetrating Europe and Asia Minor into Egypt.

III. The theory that Atlantis must be sought in the Tanzerouft, an uncharted stone desert in the south of the Sahara, has been put forward by the Frenchman Henri Lhote. Lhote has found there rock pictures and relics of a prehistoric Sahara culture which he ascribes to the Atlanteans. It is certain that the final word regarding the connection between the prehistoric culture of North Africa and the Atlantean culture has not yet been spoken. The Atlantis report asserts that Libya had been a colony of Atlantis. Numerous historical facts seem to support this statement. Egyptian sources of 3000 B.C. maintain that the Tuimah invaded North Africa and subjugated the Tehenu, who were related to the Egyptians. " Tuimah " means " North land," and this word has been written since antiquity with the island sign ⬭ , or with the ship's sign ⛵ , which is identical with the Nordic ship drawings.

The Tuimah or North island people are always shown as white-skinned, blonde-haired and blue-eyed, as represented on the wall pictures dating back to 3000 B.C. Ramses III said of the united attack of the North Sea people and the Libyans against Egypt: " The Tuimah have combined together." G. Moller rightly sees in the Tuimah of North Africa immigrants of European origin. The blonde " North people " have erected in Africa, deep in the Sahara, reputedly as many as fifty thousand graves, which in appearance and structure are identical with the megalith graves of Western and Northern Europe. In these graves there is a form of ceramics which has many features identical with the ceramics of the Northern alley graves. The Tuimah were sailors and horse and cattle breeders, just like the Atlanteans. Their rock paintings show the same technique, ornaments, (concentric half-circles, sun wheels, swastikas, etc.) as the North European rock paintings. The Tuimah, or Libyans, are always regarded by the Egyptians as being of the North people. In the battles of the thirteenth century they come under the command of the North Sea people. Like the Atlanteans, the Tuimah maintain that Poseidon was worshipped by them since "the beginning," and that he was their tribal ancestor. They also worship Atlas and the world pillar, and, like the later Teutons, know the Celts and the Philistines.

The Tuimah had chariots like the Atlanteans, and it is remarkable that the driver does not stand above the axle, as in the Egyptian chariot, but as shown on the rock paintings of Scandinavia, on the shaft of the chariot. The Tuimahs have long, straight, bronze swords and round shields, made in one piece, just like their North European allies, and no difference between them can be noticed on the rock paintings. Like them, they wear side plaits or the reed-blade crown and are dressed in a similar fashion.

Later Greek writers maintain that the Libyans were blonde; the description "*xanthos Libyos*," blonde Libyans, was a fixed description. Lucian relates that Cæsar said that nowhere on the Rhine did he find so many blonde people as in Libya. Even today many blonde, blue-eyed descendants of the "Tuimah," or North people, live in North Africa. Only few of these can be descendants of the Vandals, as the Vandals only invaded North Africa in comparatively small numbers, three thousand years after the first appearance of the blonde North people.

All these facts tend to support the statements of the Atlantis report that Libya was a colony of Atlantis, but not Atlantis itself. As we already know, it is said emphatically that Atlantis was situated outside the Pillars of Hercules, in the World Sea in the North. Its royal town stood on an island and sank in a terrible flood. These statements exclude the possibility that Atlantis was situated in the Tanzerouft, south-west of Egypt, and twelve hundred miles from the nearest sea coast. The rock paintings found there by Lhote might originate from the Atlanteans, but they are no proof that Atlantis was situated in the Sahara.

IV. W. Brandenstein has recently established a theory that Atlantis and Crete are identical, a belief which was already expressed in 1921 by the American geographer E. S. Balch.

Against this theory is the Atlantis report, which says, to repeat it once more, that Atlantis was situated outside the Pillars of Hercules, outside the straits, by which is meant the Straits of Gibraltar, a statement which does not apply to Crete. On Atlantis could be found copper in pure and melted form, and there was a great quantity of amber, which does not exist on Crete. After the catastrophes in their homeland the Atlanteans subjected Greece and Asia Minor, and penetrated as far as Egypt, an achievement which could not have been carried out by the Cretans by reason of their numbers alone. The Atlanteans possessed a strong cavalry and many chariots; on Crete, horse and cart never played an important rôle. According to the geographic ideas of that age, Atlantis was situated at the " ends of the earth," whilst Crete was, for the Egyptians and Greeks, not at the end of the earth but in an area of the sea often used by ships. After the sinking of the royal isle, an impassable and impenetrable sea of mud arose, and the channel to the open sea was blocked.

None of this applies to Crete. It is said in the *Dialogues* of Critias that the Ægean Sea was of immense depth. There had never been a sea of mud, nor was this area impassable or impenetrable. From the earliest times there had been an active traffic of ships to and from the neighbouring coasts along the Mediterranean. According to the *Odyssey* it took four days with a favourable wind to travel from Crete to Egypt. The Cretan people would have attempted to reach Egypt by way of the sea, and not crossed Greece and Asia Minor like the Atlanteans. The theory that Atlantis and Crete are identical is in direct conflict with the statements of the Atlantis report, and cannot be reconciled with historical and geographical facts.

SECTION THREE

## 1. HOMER AND THE HISTORICAL VALUE OF HIS POEM

THE wonderful poems of Homer have already led many readers to localise certain places as the scenes of the various happenings described by Homer. The poet was regarded as an almost all-knowing, godlike being, and people were convinced that in his poems he described actual happenings and places. It was not long before many islands and towns fought not only for the honour of being the poet's birthplace but also for the honour of having been the island of Circe or Calypso, the land of the Cicones or the Cyclops, or the royal isle of the Phæacians.

Later Greek scholars have dismissed all these attempts at localising the places mentioned. Eratosthenes (210 B.C.) coined the saying: " The person who wants to find the places visited by Odysseus must first find the cobbler who mended the wind-tube of Aiolos." Eratosthenes expressed this view because he thought that Homer's tales were all products of his fantasy.

This view has been shared almost universally for hundreds of years. A hundred and fifty years ago it was even thought that not only Homer's poems but the poet himself was an imaginary figure. The poems of Homer were divided into countless small parts, to which different dates were arbitrarily given, and allotted to various poets. But then Heinrich Schliemann, an enthusiastic admirer of Homer, appeared. He was convinced from the beginning that the origins of the Homeric songs were not to be found in the realms of fable but in the field of history. Schliemann was deeply convinced that the Homeric poems were not written " by themselves," or collected from a number of poets, but that they were faithful records of historical events and places by an unsurpassed poetic genius. With this conviction Schliemann dared to oppose the scientific world of his time, to scorn the hypercriticism of philologists, to put his faith in Homer's statements, and to prove with the spade the validity of his views. Schliemann had such faith in the correctness of his theory that, watch in hand, he walked the road from the headland where according to Homer the ships of the Acæans had anchored, in order to ascertain the position of the walls of Troy. He reached the conclusion, against the view of the scholars of the time, that Troy was not buried at Bunarbashi, but under the hill of Hissarlik. Here Schliemann began to dig, although the scientific world thought him foolish to take Homer's statements seriously. Schliemann found more than he himself thought possible, evidence which completely silenced the scorn of the critics; he found the ruins, walls and palaces, the temples and houses of Ilium.

The triumph of Schliemann was also the triumph of Homer, who until then had been submerged by science in a multitude of nameless poets. Homer was born again as the " true, great and immortal poet." His poems, until then dismissed as fables and fairy-tales, revealed their historical heart. The views regarding the historical value of the Homeric epics underwent such a change that an eminent historian of our time, F. Schachermeyr, could even maintain that the epics can, and indeed must, be used as historical sources, as they contain faithful records of Mycenean times, in addition to events that have been completely changed.

If in the following chapter we show greater trust in the knowledge and reliability of Homer than is usual nowadays, then we can say that we follow the path of Schliemann, whose confidence in the poet's reliability, particularly in his descriptions of places, was justified in such a singular manner.

## 2. ATLANTIS AND THE ISLAND OF THE PHÆACIANS

The Swedish scholar Olaf Rudbeck has already remarked on the striking similarity between the description of the royal town of Atlantis and that of the royal town of the Phæacians. This almost complete similarity in description has recently been frequently pointed out by, for instance, the American scholar I. Donelly and the German scholars Schulten, Henning and Kluge.

Henning said: " Between Homer's description of the land of the Phæacians, and Plato's story of Atlantis, there are so many amazing similarities that it is impossible to talk of a coincidence. There are important reasons for attributing both descriptions to one and the same source."

This original source was, according to Henning, the real conditions of Gades and Tartessos. Henning shares Schulten's view that Atlantis was situated in the south of Spain, and thinks Basileia, identical with Tartessos. As we have already seen, this view is erroneous. Basileia of the Atlantis report is identical with Basileia of Phytheas. We can therefore alter the wording of Henning and express the assumption that the single original source of the royal town of the Atlanteans and the Phæacians was the actual conditions on Basileia, the sunken royal isle near Heligoland.

How much the description of the royal island of the Atlanteans agrees with that of the Phæacians may be seen from the following parallel survey:

| The Report of Atlantis: | The Report of the land of the Phæacians: |
|---|---|
| 1. Atlantis was situated in Oceanos. | 1. The land of the Phæacians was situated in Oceanos. |
| 2. Atlantis was situated in the north. | 2. The land of the Phæacians is situated in the North. |
| 3. The Atlanteans live at the farthest end of the world. | 3. The Phæacians live at the farthest end of the world. |
| 4. Immediately before the coast of Atlantis there was a high rock island. | 4. Immediately before the coast of the land of the Phæacians there was a rock island. |

5. On the coast of Atlantis there were hills and dunes stretching to the sea.

5. On the coast of the land of the Phæacians there were hills and dunes near the sea.

6. Behind the hills and dunes there was a flat and very fertile plain.

6. Behind the hills and dunes there was the fertile plain of the land of the Phæacians.

7. The royal town of Atlantis is not situated close to the coast but about six miles inland.

7. The royal town of the land of the Phæacians is not situated near the coast, but some distance inland.

8. The royal town is surrounded by high dikes and wide water trenches.

8. The royal town is surrounded by high dikes and wide water trenches.

9. The dikes are built of earth and high enough for a ship to pass through.

9. The dikes are built of earth, and high enough for a ship to pass through.

10. In front of and behind the dikes is a harbour, but the passage is so narrow that only one ship can pass.

10. In front of and behind the dikes is a splendid harbour, but the passage is narrow.

11. A canal crosses the plain, breaking through the dikes and thus enables ships to reach the royal castle.

11. A canal crosses the plain, breaking through the dikes, thus enabling ships to reach the royal castle.

12. The buildings are constructed of stone which has been broken from the nearby rock island.

12. The buildings are erected with imported stone.

13. In the centre of the royal town lies a wonderful temple of Poseidon, and the royal castle of the highest king of Atlantis.

13. In the centre of the royal town lies a wonderful temple of Poseidon, and the royal castle of the highest king of the Phæacians.

14. The royal castle is decorated with gold, silver and copper, and is a wonderful sight. It is surrounded by a stone wall.

14. The royal castle is decorated with gold, silver and copper. It has golden and silver gates and glittering walls. It is surrounded by a wall.

15. Around the temple of Poseidon there are golden statues.

15. Around the temple of Poseidon there are golden statues.

Nordic rock drawings. Two stones from the tomb at Kivik in South Sweden

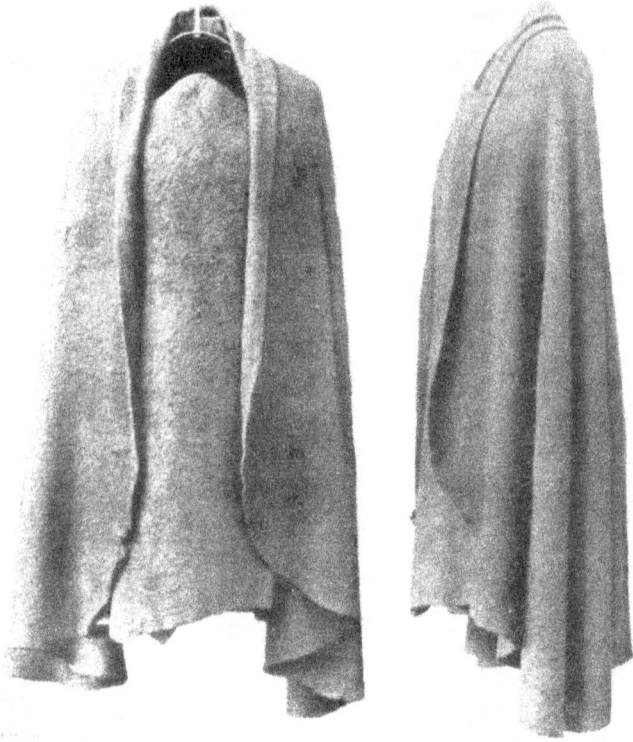

Cloak and blanket from a Danish Bronze Age grave.

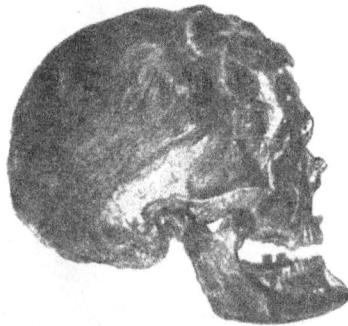

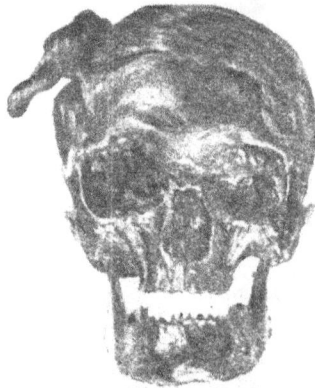

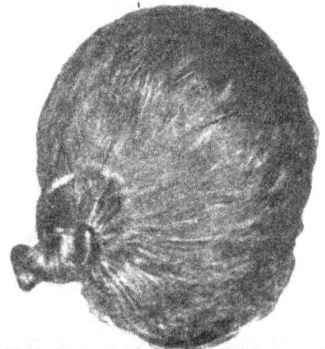

Skulls of men with side plaits from Eckernförde, Schleswig Holstein.

16. There is a gigantic statue of Poseidon, covered in gold, who is represented as the driver of winged horses, accompanied by dolphins and sea nymphs.

16. It is possible that the description of Poseidon in *Iliad* is a reminder of that Poseidon statue. Poseidon is described thus: Covered in gold, the driver of winged horses, accompanied by sea monsters.

17. Poseidon is offered by the kings of the Atlanteans great bull sacrifices. The highest king himself conducts the sacrifice.

17. Poseidon is offered by the Phæacians great bull sacrifices; the highest king himself conducts the sacrifice.

18. Near the sanctuary there is a splendid sacred wood, and an orchard of beautiful fruit trees.

18. Near the sanctuary there is a splendid sacred wood, and an orchard of beautiful fruit trees.

19. Two springs, one warm and one cold, come from there.

19. Two springs come from there.

20. The Atlanteans like bathing in warm water.

20. The Phæacians like warm baths.

21. Around the temple of Poseidon and the royal castle gatherings and sporting contests take place.

21. Around the temple of Poseidon and the royal castle gatherings and sporting contests take place.

22. In these places the Atlanteans practise gymnastics.

22. The Phæacians train in these places in boxing, ringing, jumping and in foot races.

23. Poseidon is the ancestral father of the Atlantean royal race.

23. Poseidon is the ancestral father of the Phæacian royal race.

24. One of the ancestors of the royal race of Poseidon once brought the Atlanteans to Atlantis, gathered them in a town, surrounded it with dikes, forced the inhabitants away from lawlessness and animal-like living, and trained them in the use and planting of field crops.

24. One of the ancestors of the royal race of Poseidon once brought the Phæacians to the land of the Phæacians, gathered them in a town, surrounded the town with dikes, taught the inhabitants law, built them houses and temples, and gave the people land.

25. The King of Basileia is the highest of ten kings.

25. The king of the royal isle of the Phæacians is the highest king over twelve kings.

10—A

26. The highest king is at the same time the highest priest and himself offers the bull sacrifice. The flesh of the bull is burned.

26. The highest king is also the highest priest, and himself offers the bull sacrifice. The limbs of the sacrificed bull are burned.

27. The Atlanteans are also all successors of Poseidon.

27. The Phæacians are also all successors to Poseidon.

28. The Atlanteans were superb sailors. Their great pride was their navy, consisting of twelve hundred warships.

28. The Phæacians were the finest sailors, they had the fastest ships.

29. The Atlanteans had " ship houses."

29. The Phæacians had " boat houses."

30. The Atlanteans were especially favoured by the gods.

30. The Phæacians were very much favoured by the gods, they were of a godlike nature.

31. They were once unmixed by the blood of other mortals.

31. They had nothing in common with anybody.

32. The climate on Atlantis was especially favourable. A soft west wind blew continually and the harvest was brought in twice a year.

32. The climate on the Phæacian land was particularly favourable. The harvest could be gathered twice a year.

This parallel survey shows clearly that Atlantis and the land of the Phæacians were identical. The conformity in the descriptions of both islands is so convincing and also so great in minor matters that the suspicion may arise that Homer knew the Atlantis report and used it as a model for his story about the Phæacians. The following reasons oppose this theory:

1. Homer gives a whole string of details about the Phæacian land which are not contained in the Atlantis report, but which do not come from his imagination as they describe actual conditions. For example, Homer gives precise sailing directions to the Phæacian land. He tells of a stream at the river mouth, and he reports that the dikes around the royal town were protected by pillars. Homer also wrote down a number of legends which in all probability originate from the Nordic area. The Atlantis report says nothing of these matters. The valuable additional material

which Homer gives in addition to the Atlantis report proves that he had other sources than the report.

2. On the other hand, the Atlantis report contains information which is not found in Homer, and which would undoubtedly have been used by a poet if he had known about it. The Atlantis report mentions, for example, rich deposits of amber on Basileia; it mentions that copper was found there in pure and melted form; that the rock on the island of Basileia consisted of red, white and black stone, and that walls and buildings were built of multi-coloured stone to please the eye. The Atlantis report also mentions in detail the preparation of the assembly of the kings, and the solemn procedures which occurred during the bull sacrifice. Homer knows nothing of all these details, although he writes of the wealth of the Phæacians, the high rock island before the Phæacian land where the kings gathered for law-giving and a great bull sacrifice.

3. The independence of the Atlantis report and the Phæacians from each other is underlined by the differences in both descriptions.

In the Atlantis report the great military force, the weapons and army organisation of the Atlanteans are described in detail. Their destructive wars against Greece, Asia Minor and Egypt are mentioned, but in the Phæacian report the Phæacians are described as a peace-loving people who do not care for " bows and arrows." A war against Greece and Asia Minor is therefore quite out of the question. The Atlantis report describes the frightful catastrophe of the destruction of Basileia and its serious consequences. Homer reports nothing of this misfortune, although he describes the Phæacians in such a way that the inhabitants of that country are first met after the sinking of their islands. The Atlantis report mentions in detail the heroic struggle of Athens against the Atlanteans, and it seems unlikely that Homer, had he known it, would have kept quiet about a story of such importance to the Greeks.

4. Plato emphasises that Solon, when he heard the Atlantis report, declared that neither he nor any other Greek knew anything about these happenings. The Atlantis

report was, therefore, unknown in Greece before Solon. Homer, who lived without doubt several centuries before Solon, could not have known a report brought back by Solon.

For all these reasons we must conclude that both reports are quite independent of each other. The many surprising similarities have come about because in both reports the same country is described; but not because one report was the model for the other.

We thus possess two reports about Basileia independent of each other. Both confirm and complement each other and present us with a remarkable picture of the life and customs of the inhabitants of the sunken land of the West more than three thousand years ago.

### 3.   SAILING DIRECTIONS TO BASILEIA

In order to show the remarkable knowledge which Homer had about the sunken royal island near Heligoland, it is easiest if we accompany Odysseus on his voyage to the Phæacian land, and during the events in the royal town of the Phæacians.

After having spent seven years on the lonely island of Ogygia with the goddess Calypso, Odysseus was told to journey to the land of the Phæacians.

Homeric scholars have repeatedly expressed astonishment that the *Odyssey* contained sailing directions which read rather like log books, which must have already been in use in those days. Seemingly Homer must have used as models log books, or sailing manuals, called *Periplus* in Greek, which gave the exact course and distance between the different islands and coasts. The courses were given by star constellations, or prevailing wind directions. Henning said about these sailing directions: " They are of such marvellous precision, that even today any sailor could keep an exact course by following them." They are one of the strongest proofs that Homer drew his descriptions from real life, and not from fantasy. The sailing directions read as follows:

It was with a happy heart that the good Odysseus spread his sail to catch the wind and used his seamanship to keep his boat straight with the steering-oar. There he sat and never closed his eyes in sleep, but kept them on the Pleiads, or watched Bootes slowly set, or the Great Bear, nicknamed the Wain, which always wheels round in the same place and looks across at Orion the Hunter with a wary eye. It was this constellation, the only one which never bathes in Ocean's stream, that the wise goddess Calypso had told him to keep on his left hand as he made across the sea. So for seventeen days he sailed on his course, and on the eighteenth there hove into sight the shadowy mountains of the Phæacians' country, which jutted out to meet him there. The land looked like a shield laid on the misty sea.*

In order to test the nautical value of the sailing instructions it is necessary to determine the starting point of this voyage.

Before starting his journey, Odysseus had been with the goddess Calypso on the island Ogygia, which was uninhabited and was situated in the endless wilderness of Oceanos. The island of Ogygia was also called the " navel of the sea." The goddess lived in a large cave on the island.

Ancient Greek scholars emphasised long ago that the island of Ogygia must have been in the World Ocean. Strabo also declares that the voyage of Odysseus must have taken place in the World Ocean.

Outside the Pillars of Hercules (Gibraltar), called by Homer Scylla and Charybdis, there are three main groups of islands: the Canary Islands, Madeira and the Azores. All three groups have been identified with Ogygia.

The following reasons speak against the identification of Ogygia with the Canaries or Madeira:

1. It has been repeatedly said of Ogygia that the island was uninhabited. The Canaries and Madeira, however, have been populated since the earliest Stone Age. These islands were actually areas of retreat for the Cromagnon people and kept their early Stone Age cultures until their rediscovery in the Middle Ages.

2. Odysseus was told to steer in one night towards Bootes and Pleiades. According to the calculations of Dr. Villinger,

*Homer: *The Odyssey*, Book V, page 94. Penguin Classics. Translated by E. V. Rieu.

these two constellations are not visible on the same night during the summer, when Odysseus undertook his travels, south of the 35th degree of latitude. If this astronomical direction is to make sense, Odysseus must have been on an island of the World Ocean north of the 35th degree of latitude. But there are only the Azores; Madeira and the Canaries are south of the 35th degree of latitude.

If we are to take the statements of Homer seriously, there remains of the islands in the World Ocean only one island of the Azores which could be identified with Ogygia. Homer says the following about Ogygia:

1. After a nine days' voyage Odysseus reached Ogygia during the tenth night after having passed Scylla and Charybdis. Henning has proved with many striking arguments that the rocks of Scylla and Charybdis can be identified with the rocks of the Straits of Gibraltar.

2. Ogygia is called by Homer the " navel of the sea." This is the ancient name for the island of St. Miguel. In the eighteenth century this island was still called " *umbilicus maris*," " navel of the sea."

3. According to Homer's description, there was a great cave on Ogygia in which lived the goddess Calypso. It seems that Homer knew something of a cave sanctuary on that island.

There is in fact a great cave on St. Miguel which evidently housed in prehistoric times an ancient sanctuary. When the Azores were rediscovered by the Portuguese in the fifteenth century a stone plate was found in this cave with the picture of a building which was regarded by Le Cour as a picture of an Atlantean temple. Furthermore, rock paintings were discovered which are reminiscent of Nordic runes but which could not be deciphered, as well as a statue of a horse rider in a good state of preservation. Unfortunately these finds were lost *en route* when they were transported to Portugal by order of the Portuguese king around 1550.

4. According to Plutarch, Ogygia was situated in the wide desert of the sea, five days to the west of the British Isles. Plutarch knew the great cave on Ogygia. He said that

Cronos, the first king of Atlantis, slept there with his companions, a legend which according to Grimm and Welcker sounds like an ancient Teutonic legend about the sleeping kings in mountain caves, and seems to be of Nordic origin. Even though Plutarch's statement about the position of Ogygia is not quite correct, as the Azores are to the south-west, and not the west, of the British Isles, it still shows that Ogygia can only be identified with the most northern island of the island groups of the World Ocean in question. Plutarch's statement fits the Azores best. His tale, that in the cave of Ogygia slept Cronos, a king of Atlantis, shows like the statement of Homer that the goddess of Ogygia was a daughter of Atlas, and that long ago in the past it was believed that this island was somehow related to Atlas and Atlantis. That is why in our time it has often been thought that Atlantis must have been situated near the Azores.

Coins of Carthaginian origin dating back to the sixth or seventh century B.C. show how early the Azores must have been located. Other prehistoric finds, attributed earlier to the Phœnicians, are recognised by Donelly as relics of the Atlanteans, who must have had a cave sanctuary there.

Even though the Azores were not inhabited in antiquity, these various finds show that occasionally sailors, ship-wrecked perhaps, like Odysseus, set foot on the islands.

It is quite possible that Homer was following the log book of a man who knew the position of the Azores and their particular conditions.

We have, therefore, many reasons for identifying the island of Ogygia with the Azores island St. Miguel, and shall take it as the starting point for the voyage of Odysseus.

Odysseus was charged by the goddess Calypso to proceed immediately after the rise of Bootes and Pleiades. According to Henning, Bootes and Pleiades rose at an almost exact mathematical point in the east–north-east. On this course Odysseus navigated from St. Miguel straight through the English Channel into the North Sea towards the island of Heligoland.

The voyage took seventeen days, aided by a most favourable wind which was sent by the goddess herself. During the eighteenth day Odysseus saw the rock island appear in front of the Phæacian coast. We see that Henning was evidently right to speak of the wonderful precision of Calypso's sailing directions.

A good sailing direction also needs a graphic description of the point and coast aimed at. For this reason we always find in ancient and modern sailing manuals descriptions or outlines of the destined country. In the sailing direction to the land of the Phæacians such an outline of the coast of Basileia is also given. It says there that " the land looked like a shield laid on the misty sea."

A shield is a flat plain, in the centre of which rises a shield umbo. It can easily be seen that by this description is meant the contours of Heligoland and the hills behind it, or the dunes of Basileia. Heligoland is the shield umbo which lay in the centre of the Atlantis-Phæacian land, which extended beyond the edges by about sixty feet. The contours of this coastal sector must have really looked from the west–south-west, the course of approach of Odysseus, like a shield in the misty sea.

The following verses prove that Odysseus did actually approach this rock island. In the immediate vicinity of the coast, Poseidon, who was angry with Odysseus, discovered the hero, and destroyed his boat by a thunderstorm. Odysseus was thrown on to the rock island. Then follows an impressive description of the island:

> But when he had come within call of the shore, he heard the thunder of surf on a rocky coast. With an angry roar the great seas were battering at the ironbound land and all was veiled in spray. There were no coves, no harbours that would hold a ship; nothing but headlands jutting out, sheer rock, and jagged reefs. When he realised this, Odysseus' knees quaked and his courage ebbed. He groaned in misery as he summed up the situation to himself:
> " When I had given up hope, Zeus let me see the land, and I have taken all the trouble to swim to it across those leagues of water, only to find no way whatever of getting out of this grey surf and making my escape. Off shore, the pointed reefs

set in a raging sea; behind, a smooth cliff rising sheer; deep water near in; and never a spot where a man could stand on both his feet and get to safety. If I try to land, I may be lifted by a roller and dashed against the solid rock—in which case I'd have had my trouble for nothing. While, if I swim farther down the coast on the chance of finding a natural harbour where the beaches take the waves aslant, it is only too likely that another squall will pounce on me and drive me out to join the deep-sea fish, where all my groans would do no good. Or some monster might be inspired to attack me from the depths. Amphitrite has a name for mothering plenty of such creatures in her seas; and I am well aware how the great Earthshaker detests me."

This inward debate was cut short by a tremendous wave which swept him forward to the rugged shore, where he would have been flayed and all his bones been broken, had not the bright-eyed goddess Athene put it into his head to dash in and lay hold of a rock with both his hands. He clung there groaning while the great wave marched by. But no sooner had he escaped its fury than it struck him once more with the full force of its backward rush and flung him far out to sea. Pieces of skin stripped from his sturdy hands were left sticking to the crag, thick as the pebbles that stick to the suckers of a squid when he is torn from his hole. The great surge passed over Odysseus' head and there the unhappy man would have come to an unpredestined end, if Athene had not inspired him with a wise idea. Getting clear of the coastal breakers as he struggled to the surface, he now swam along outside them, keeping an eye on the land, in the hope of lighting on some natural harbour with shelving beaches. Presently his progress brought him off the mouth of a fast-running stream and it struck him that this was the best spot he could find, for it was not only clear of rocks but sheltered from the winds. The current told him that he was at a river's mouth. . . .*

Never again has the " sheer rising cliff " of Heligoland been more vividly described in the roaring of a North Sea storm as in these verses of Homer. The " smooth, rising cliffs," the " pointed reefs " of these verses are in complete agreement with the actual conditions.

* Homer: *The Odyssey*, Book V, page 98. Penguin Classics. Translated by E. V. Rieu.

The poet believed that the river ran from east to west. There can be no doubt that he describes here the River Eider. Its mouth really was in those days immediately south of Heligoland in the North Sea, its course ran from east to west.

Before Odysseus could set foot on the land the following happened. Even though Odysseus saw the smooth, stoneless bank of the river, and the tide was carrying him into the river mouth, the tide now changed and it was impossible for Odysseus to reach the bank. He prayed to the river god and a miracle happened: the god stopped the current to the sea, and Odysseus was carried safely to the river bank. Henning says at this point: Krummel has already stressed in 1902 that in Book V of the *Odyssey* the appearance of the flood-tide in the river was described. He writes that it must have appeared a miracle to the Greek that a river could flow upstream at its mouth. To such a miracle the hero Odysseus owes his lucky landing on the Phæacian island, because after his prayer for mercy, the river god stopped the floods and saved him on the soft river bank.

Tidal floods in river mouths are unknown in the whole Mediterranean area. Henning adds that this remark is of decisive importance. No other fact lends as much weight to the supposition that Homer was picturing a real river. Henning thinks it quite impossible that from poetic inspiration alone the Greek would describe geographical facts, like the tidal floods in river mouths. This point alone can be seen as proof that the description of the Phæacian land is not a product of the imagination; the poet must have been in possession of unexpectedly precise and appropriate descriptions of conditions prevailing in the Oceanic West. If we consider that Pytheas, four centuries after Homer, was the first Greek to recognise the low and high tides of the sea, and to study the flood tide, the flood tide wave in the fifth song of the *Odyssey* is the more astonishing.

From all these observations we see that the assumption that Homer must have had access to log books for his voyage cannot be dismissed. The sailing instructions to the land of the Phæacians, the description of the high rock island before

Basileia, the details of the great river running through the Phæacian country, agree with reality to such a degree that this agreement cannot be ascribed to poetic inspiration, but only to the use of a sea log book or sailing manual.

### 4.  DESCRIPTION OF THE PHÆACIAN COUNTRY

One of the most charming of Odysseus' experiences during his ten years of wandering is his meeting with Nausicaa, the daughter of the Phæacian king Alcinous. These scenes have been embellished by Homer with loving care. In this case we are not interested in the embellishment, but in the source used by Homer for the description of the royal isle. The statements made by the poet show that he must have had remarkable knowledge about the island.

After having reached the river bank Odysseus, as promised, threw the veil of Ino, who had saved him, into the river.

Radermacher has pointed out that this passage is reminiscent of the ancient Nordic legends, where the veil of a sea nymph also saves the hero. Perhaps an ancient Nordic legend has been woven by Homer into his poem.

Then the hero, tired to death, climbs the hills which spread out along the river bank. These hills near the water are also mentioned in the Atlantis report. Perhaps the diluvian high lands are meant here which surrounded the island of Basileia. For the description of these hills Homer used the rare Greek word " *klitys*," which is closely connected with the ancient Danish word " *klit*." Behind these hills Odysseus can see the flat, rich land of the Phæacians. The royal town, however, is too distant to be seen by Odysseus. The hero falls asleep through exhaustion and sleeps until the afternoon of the following day. He is woken up by the clamour of the Phæacian maidens playing on the river bank; he discloses his identity and asks for clothing and help. After Nausicaa promises him help and clothing, Odysseus washes off the salt on his body in the river. At this time the river must have consisted of fresh water, because one cannot wash salt off with sea water. Odysseus then follows the maidens in the carriage of Nausicaa, who drives hurriedly towards the distant royal town. Eventually Nausicaa and her retinue reach the high dikes surrounding the royal town. We shall hear later about the construction of these dikes. Before and behind the dikes was a splendid harbour; the passage through the dikes was narrow, just as was reported of the dikes on Basileia. The towers, gates and bridges mentioned in the Atlantis report are not mentioned by Homer; possibly his sources did not describe these structures. In the verses that follow the various places in the royal town of the Phæacians are described just as in the Atlantis report. Homer tells of the temple of Poseidon surrounded by the market place, of the royal castle near the temple, of the sacred wood, the two springs, the places of sporting contests, the shipbuilding yards and the boat-houses of the Phæacians, just as described in the Atlantis report. Even with these descriptions it is obvious that Homer did not use the Atlantis report as a basis, but that the agreements have come about because both descriptions reproduce the real conditions on Basileia.

### 5. THE SHIPPING OF THE PHÆACIANS

Homer praised highly the shipbuilding skill of the Phæacians and their familiarity with navigational matters. He said that they only cared for fast, agile ships, and asserted that all their men knew how to handle ships.

The details reported by Homer about the shipbuilding skill of the Phæacians make it apparent that he must have used reliable reports for his facts. He relates that the Phæacians had boat-houses for their sea vessels. This is said of no other nation in Homer's epic. The Atlantis report also talks of the " *neosoikoi* " of the Atlanteans, in which large animals could be housed. Although in this connection the report mentions mainly ships' bunkers on the nearby rock island, that does not exclude the possibility that boat-houses were also erected on Basileia proper.

The ships of the Phæacians are described by Homer as double-tailed. This epithet becomes clearer as soon as we look at the ships of the North people, who are identical with the Phæacians, on the Egyptian reliefs in Medinet Habu and the Scandinavian rock paintings of the Bronze Age. On the reliefs and rock paintings, the ships of the North people are equipped with a rising, tailed stem at bow and stern, and are therefore actually " double-tailed."

The ships of the Phæacians carry, according to Homer, a mast which can be lowered. On the wall pictures of Medinet Habu, similarly, some of the North ships have a lowered mast; none of the Egyptian ships are represented thus. Homer related that the Phæacians set their sails. The wall pictures in Medinet Habu show that the North people had a special technique for setting sails. The sails are only travelled with one square sail; the lower sail, the " tree," is left out. Koster came to the same view as Homer when, looking at the warships of the North people on the Egyptian reliefs, he said that the North people were the most experienced sailors of the world during the time of Ramses III. The technique of unfurling the sails displayed on the Egyptian reliefs has lasted until the present time, and the sails of small fishing vessels are still used in this way.

Homer reports that the Phæacians anchored their ships by means of a pierced stone. Such stone anchors were also used in the North during the age of the Vikings, until they were replaced by metal anchors. The names given by Homer to individual Phæacians show the enthusiasm of the Phæacians for sailing.

### 6. THE FORMATION OF THE COAST DUNES IN PHÆCIA

Homer reports that the wide ocean gave the Phæacians not only pleasure but also serious anxieties. Poseidon said " I propose to wreck that fine ship of the Phæacians on the high seas as she comes back from her mission, to teach them to hold their hands and give up this habit of escorting travellers. And I will also fence their town with a ring of high mountains."*

The first part of this threat was carried out, because near the coast Poseidon changed the large ship into a shiplike

* Homer: *The Odyssey.* p. 212. Penguin Classics. Translated by E. V. Rieu.

rock. The Phæacians were then worried lest Poseidon would also carry out the second threat and create mountains around the town.

The anxiety of the Phæacians about the " mountains of Poseidon " can only be justified if these mountains are a danger to their fertile land and to their shipping. Evidently what is meant here is the threat of wandering dunes which cover the " fat land of the Phæacians " with sand and block their harbours. It may have been that the fields and harbour installations of the Phæacians were threatened by wandering dunes. How acute the danger of wandering sand dunes was in the sea area around Basileia can be seen from the example of the island of Trieschen, on the west coast of Northern Germany, where fertile marshland was completely covered in a few years by wandering dunes. When these dunes, which had protected the land from the sea, moved on, the sea had free access to the land and destroyed it to such an extent that only the remains were left. Something similar must have happened on Basileia.

## 7. SPORTS IN PHÆACIA

Just as the Atlantis report talks of the liking of the Atlanteans for sport and games, so Homer talks of the love of the Phæacians for sport, competitions and physical exercises. Alcinous, the King of the Phæacians, says to his subjects: " Let us go out of doors now and try our hands at various sports, so that when our guest has reached his home he can tell his friends that at boxing, wrestling, jumping and running there is no one who could beat us."*

Sporting contests were held in many places in Phæacia. Umpires supervised the games, and the racecourses were surrounded by a multitude of people.

Of the sports events special mention is made of discus throwing with a stone discus as well as a special ball game. Finds of stone discs prove that in the Bronze Age there were also great stone discs which had been used by the Phæacians during their competitions. The ball game at which the

* Homer: *The Odyssey*, p. 126. Penguin Classics. Translated by E. V. Rieu.

Phæacians showed great skill filled Odysseus with admiration; he had seen nothing like it anywhere.

These ball games were also popular later in the Teutonic North. Just as the Phæacians held their game in honour of Odysseus, so it was the custom later in the North to hold games in honour of an important guest. As with the Phæacians, they were played between two sides.

## 8. THE RITUAL DANCE OF THE PHÆACIANS

When we discussed the strange castle of Basileia and heard of the ancient legend that Poseidon himself planned it in order to keep Cleito in captivity, we came to the conclusion that it was a very ancient Trojan castle which was probably erected in the Stone Age or later Bronze Age. In many of these Trojan castles ritual dances took place which were probably meant to influence the course of the sun. The Atlantis report does not mention such a dance on Basileia, although one might have expected it. Homer however, who called this dance a " divine dance," has handed down to us such a dance on Basileia. In honour of Odysseus the King of the Phæacians called on chosen young men who were specially skilled in this dance. We are told that the spot upon which the dance took place was measured and flattened, and that nine stewards also supervised the dance.

> Meanwhile the equerry came up to Demodocus and handed him his tuneful lyre. The minstrel then moved forward to the centre; a band of expert dancers, all in the first bloom of youth, took up their positions round him; and their feet came down on the sacred floor with a scintillating movement that filled Odysseus with admiration as he watched.*

Many centuries later Tacitus reported similar dances by young men of the Teutons. They still took place in Germany as late as the Middle Ages.

* Penguin Classics, *Ibid.*, p. 130.

### 9.  WEAVING SKILLS OF THE PHÆACIANS

Homer says this about the Phæacian women:

> Some grind the apple-golden corn in the handmill, some weave at the loom, or sit and twist the yarn, their hands fluttering like the tall poplar's leaves, while the soft olive-oil drips from the close-woven fabrics they have finished. For the Phæacians' extraordinary skill in handling ships at sea is rivalled by the dexterity of their womenfolk at the loom, so expert has Athene made them in the finer crafts, and so intelligent.*

Among other valuable presents Odysseus was given a wonderful linen cloth. The great skill of Teuton women of the Bronze Age in weaving, plaiting, and knitting has repeatedly been mentioned. That the North people very early on gained a reputation for the making of linen cloths can be seen from the Egyptian description " Tuimah," or " Tamahu," by which the North people were also described. " *Ta mah* " means " *North land.*" Brugscj has proved that the Egyptians called cloth " *mah*," and the land of cloths " *ta mah.* The word used for the North land, " *Ta mah* " actually means " land of the linen plant."

It is also worth noticing that Ramses III painted the North Sea people and their allies with a linen plant to indicate their Nordic origin, or their belonging to the North army. This was perhaps a sign that linen or flax was a plant typical of, and cultivated by, the North Sea peoples.

These observations show that Homer was right in praising the great skill of the Nordic women in the art of weaving, and in the making of valuable woollen or linen garments.

Many other details of the Phæacians described by Homer were probably correctly observed. For example, he reports that the Phæacians passed food and drink to the right, a custom still strictly observed in Northern Friesland, which probably originated in the worship of the sun's rightward motion, and therefore dates from the Bronze Age.

The Eighth Song of the *Odyssey* relates that the Phæacians

* Penguin Classics, *Ibid.*, p. 115.

Gold vessels found on Borgbjerg hill on the Danish island of Zealand.

A lump of pure copper from Heligoland.

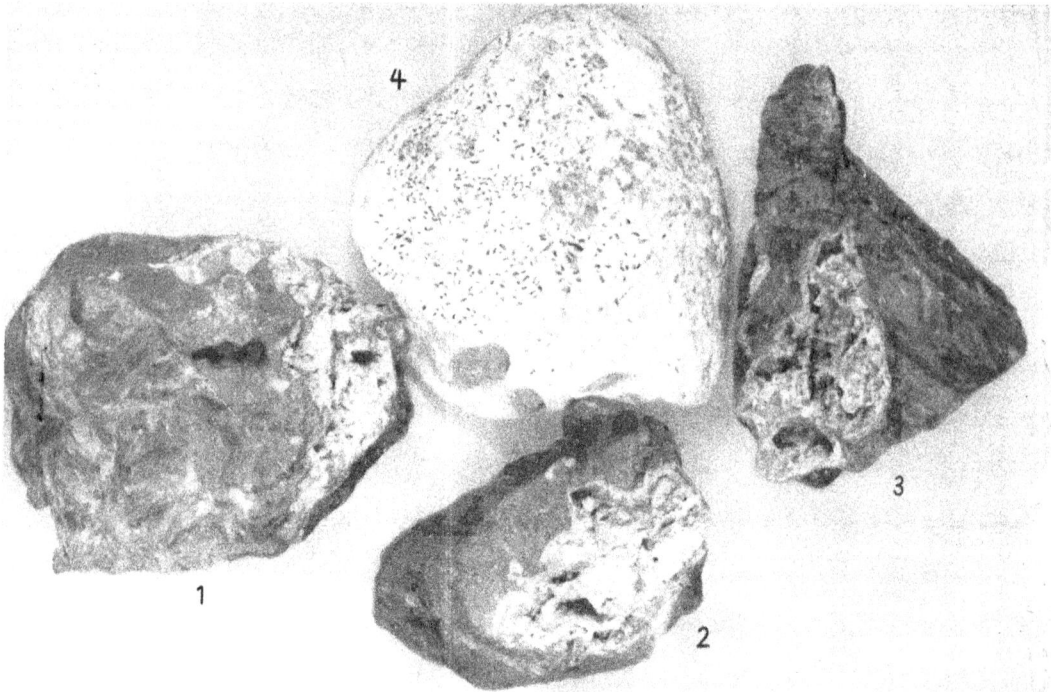

Stones from Heligoland. 1–3 copper druses in coloured sandtone, 4 limestone from the " White Cliff.'

prepared a warm bath for Odysseus and then took a meal with him. Every participant had his own table and chair. The same is reported by Tacitus about the Teutons: " After the bath they ate, when everyone had his own table and chair." Greeks and Romans used to sit during their meals at a communal table.

The meals of the Phæacians evidently took place at the open fireside. This is also reported of the Teutons by Tacitus. It was not the custom with Mediterranean peoples on account of the warm climate. Golden goblets, golden tankards and a brass kettle were used in the castle of the Phæacian king. Similar vessels are known from Bronze Age finds in the Nordic area.

Lute and harp playing were known to the Phæacians. The same is said by Greek writers of the Hyperboreoi, who were, without doubt, identical with the Atlanteans. The instrument was probably a *hrotta*, which is still used nowadays in Sweden under the name " forest harp," or the " win," or " winne," an instrument like the lute which is still played in the North.

If such instruments have not been preserved for us from the Nordic Bronze Age, the numerous " lures " known to us from the Nordic area show that the making of musical instruments, probably also composition, must have been highly developed there.

The place of honour in the king's hall was " near the hearth, at the great pillar, in the centre of the hall." The same was the case in later times with the Teutons, and this arrangement is still in use nowadays in the North Friesian area.

The royal house of the Phæacians described by Homer was probably a so-called " ridge pillar house," a house supported by pillars. This kind of building was already known in the Nordic area during the Bronze Age. The house of the Philistine king in Gaza, the roof of which collapsed when Samson tore away the two pillars, must also have been a ridge pillar house. An eminent scholar was able to prove astonishing similarities between the ancient Nordic and Philistine methods of house building.

According to Homer's descriptions the Phæacians wore coat and frock. Such coats and frocks, or blouses, are known from original finds of the Bronze Age. Tacitus described them as the customary garment of the Teutons during his time.

The King of the Phæacians speaks of three stubborn sisters who spin the life thread of the people. This is apparently an allusion to the three Norns, who, according to later Teutonic beliefs, spin and cut the life thread of man.

Nowhere else did Odysseus enjoy similar hospitality; both Nausicaa and the " grey hero Echeneus " regarded it as a sacred duty to offer hospitality to the stranger. This reminds us of the words of Tacitus: " To deny any stranger shelter is regarded by the Teutons as sin. Everyone looks after his guest as best as he can." The description of the banquet in the house of the Phæacian king is reminiscent of the " feasting " of the ancient Teutons.

The verses concerning Phæacia seem to carry little weight in details, but as a whole they convey the impression that Homer must have used excellent sources for them. Not only do the general remarks about the Nordic islands and their inhabitants withstand critical examination, but many minor comments on the formation of dunes, boat-houses, skill in weaving, etc., also appear to be historically correct. As most of these statements are not contained in the Atlantis report we have further support for the assumption that Homer did not use the report, but some other reliable source. Moreover, according to the Roman chronicler Tacitus, some maintain that Odysseus, on his long, legendary wanderings was driven towards the Nordic ocean and there set foot on Teutonic soil.

AS we have already seen, after its destruction the amber island went into the legends of the people living near the North Sea as " fields of amber," " glass tower," " glass house," etc. In all the legends the amber island is described as the " island of the blessed," or the " island of the dead."

The oldest written record of this legend can be found in the ancient Greek legends of the Hyperboreoi. The classical philologist Schroder has proved that this legend originated during the earliest period of Greek settlement, in the twelfth and eleventh century B.C., and was probably brought by the North people themselves to Greece. According to tradition the Hyperboreoi lived in the Northern Ocean, on the amber coast. The amber river Eridanus, or Eider, ran through the country. The Hyperborean land stretched from south to north, longer than Sicily, and an impenetrable sea of mud lay before its coast.

There can be no doubt that the " Hyperborean land " is the same as the Cymbrian peninsula.

In the legends of the Hyperboreoi it is said that a ship of the dead lies ready at the coast in order to bring the dead to the island of the blessed. According to the ancient commentator Tzetze many Greek poets and writers—Hesiod, Homer, Lycophron, Plutarch, Philostratos, Dion and others —have taken from this Nordic legend the story of the island of the blessed and the ferrymen who take the dead across. Procop (sixth century A.D.) also speaks in his " Gothic Wars " of the islands of the blessed in the North Sea, and of the ferrymen of the dead who carry the blessed across. These legends are still alive today on the North Sea coast. The most impressive is the ancient Frisian tradition of the crossing of the souls of the dead to " white Aland," which can be identified with the sunken Atlantis.

According to this ancient Frisian legend, it has been the custom of the North Sea coast since time immemorial to hire certain fishermen to ferry the souls of the dead during the deepest night to " white Aland." These fishermen had to keep their ships prepared during the darkest night of the year. In complete darkness the souls of the departed were brought on board. When the ship was fully laden the voyage began against wind and waves, " quicker than a bird " to the island of the dead. The fishermen did not have to know the way as the ships steered the course by themselves. The journey went on in complete silence " and nothing could be heard but a whisper, as if mice were rustling in the straw." When " white Aland " was reached the ship was unloaded and the souls brought on land. Then the ships raced back because they had to be back at their starting point when dawn broke.

The scholar Frederick Welcker was struck by the similarity of the description of the Phæacians by Homer to the ferrymen of the dead of the Hyperborean legend, and he maintained that the Phæacians originated from the Hyperborean legend, and that their origin must be found in the Hyperborean area.

We have seen that Homer knew much more about the North Sea than just this legend. The notion that at the end of the second millennium B.C. the North Sea area was a world on its own of which the people of the Mediterranean had no knowledge can no longer be supported. The amber trade alone, which brought the " gold of the North " throughout the second millennium B.C. in great quantity to the Mediterranean areas, and particularly the immigration of the North Sea people around 1200 B.C. into the South-Eastern areas, certainly brought knowledge of the North Sea and also many legends and myths to the South.

The correctness of Welcker's theory can best be proved by a comparison between the statement made by Homer about the Phæacians and the Nordic traditions about the ferrymen of the dead. The King of the Phæacians says to Odysseus:

> Tell me the name by which you were known at home to your mother and father and your friends in the town and country round. You must also tell me where you come from, to what state and to what city you belong, so that my ships as they convey you there may plan the right course in their minds. For the Phæacians have no steersmen, nor steering-oars such as other craft possess. Our ships know by instinct what their crews are thinking and propose to do. They know every city, every fertile land, and hidden in mist and cloud they make their swift passage over the sea's immensities with no fear of damage and no thought of wreck.*

In the Thirteenth Song of Odysseus it says:

> When they had come down to the ship and the sea, the young nobles who were to escort him took charge of his baggage, including all the food and drink, and stowed it in the hold. For Odysseus himself they spread a rug and sheet on the ship's deck, well aft, so that he might enjoy unbroken sleep. Then he too climbed on board and quietly lay down, while the crew found their seats on the benches like men drilled to their work and untied the cable from the pierced stone that held it. But no sooner had they swung back and struck the water with their blades than sweet oblivion sealed Odysseus' eyes in sleep delicious and profound, the very counterfeit of death. And now, like a team of four stallions on the plain who start as one horse at the touch of the whip and break into their bounding stride to make short work of the course, the ship lunged forward, and above the great dark wave that the sea sent roaring in her wake her stern began to rise and fall. With unfaltering speed she forged ahead, and not even the wheeling falcon, the fastest thing that flies, could have kept her company. Thus she sped lightly on, cutting her way through the waves and carrying a man wise as the gods are wise, who in long years of war on land and wandering across the cruel seas had suffered many agonies of spirit but now was lapped in peaceful sleep, forgetting all he had once endured.

When the brightest of all stars came up, the star which often

* Penguin Classics, *Ibid* p. 139.

ushers in the tender light of Dawn, the ship's voyage was done and she drew near to Ithaca. Now in that island is a cove named after Phorcys, the Old Man of the Sea, with two bold headlands squatting at its mouth so as to protect it from the heavy swell raised by rough weather in the open and allow large ships to ride inside without so much as tying up, once within mooring distance of the shore.

In the Seventh Song of the *Odyssey* it is told how the Phæacians took Rhadamanthus, the judge on the Island of the Dead, with them on their ships across the sea and returned him home again in one day. This statement caused the ancient interpreter of the Homeric epics to declare that the land of the Phæacians and the Island of the Dead must have been situated in the same neighbourhood.

A comparison of Homer's story about the Phæacians with the stories of the Nordic legend of the Driver of the Dead show that both must have been without doubt identical.

1. It has been said against Welcker's theory that the Phæacians were identical with the Drivers of the Dead, that the Phæacians are described by Homer as people of flesh and blood, and therefore cannot be identified with the Drivers of the Dead, who must have been a creation of fantasy. But the Drivers of the Dead in the Nordic legend were in fact people of flesh and blood; the old Frisian legend even gives the name of one: he was called Jan Hugen, had a wife and children, and occupied himself as a fisherman. Procop also tells of the Drivers of the Dead in the North Sea, their fishing, agriculture and shipping, and that they were subjects of the Franks. We have here complete agreement between the statements of Homer and the Nordic legend.

2. The very name given by Homer to the inhabitants of Basileia, Phæacian, is a reminder of the " black drivers " of the Nordic legend. The name Phæacian derives from the Greek word " *phaios*," meaning " black," and signifies in particular the colour of death and sorrow. " *Phaiacoi* " means also literally the " black." Homer calls these " blacks " " *pompoi apemones hapanton*," " the safe escorts of all." The Phæacians of Homer are therefore in the literal translation, " black escorts," just as in the Nordic legend.

Homer also mentions that the ships of the Phæacians are black, as well as their sails and the crew.

3. According to Homer these "black escorts" fly "quicker than thoughts," "quicker than hawks," across the seas. The same is said of the Nordic escorts of the Dead. They also fly quicker than the bird, or the storm wind across the seas; they suddenly appear out of the sea and disappear again in a flash. According to Procop, the Nordic escorts of the Dead could cover in an hour a distance which would take normal ships one day and one night.

4. Homer says that the ships of the Phæacians did not require steersmen and rudders, but found their way "by themselves in night and fog." Exactly the same is told of the Nordic escort ships of the Dead.

5. Homer says that the voyage of the Phæacian ship was carried out in deepest silence. The same is said of the voyage of the Nordic escort ship of the Dead. The souls of the Dead remain in complete silence. Not a word is spoken on board the ship, and nothing is heard but a whisper as if mice were rustling in the straw.

6. Homer says that the stormy sea could neither damage nor swallow the ships of the Phæacians. The escort ships of the Dead in the Nordic legend cannot be damaged by storm or bad weather, and the biggest waves can do no harm. On the contrary, the wilder the storm and the higher the waves, the quicker the black escorts of the Dead hurry across the ocean.

7. The final proof that the Phæacians were in fact the escorts of the Dead of the Nordic legend is given by Homer himself, when he tells how the Phæacians took Rhadamanthus, the king and judge on the Island of the Dead, across the sea to Greece, and back again to the Island of the Dead. With regard to this point, the ancient Greek grammarians said that the Isle of the Blessed must have been in the vicinity of the Island of the Phæacians, whilst more recent investigators have declared on the basis of Homer's statements that the Island of the Blessed must be identical with the Island of the Phæacians.

This conclusion is without doubt correct. We have already seen previously that this island went into the legend of the

North Sea people after its destruction as the " Isle of the Dead," the " land of the Blessed under the Waves," " *glasis vellir*," or " fields of amber," or as *Abalus*, or Isle of the Dead.

In his tale of the Phæacians Homer has woven a legend from the North Sea area into his immortal verses.

### 2. THE LEGEND OF THE LÆSTRYGONIANS

The legend of the escorts of the Dead, which has been told by Homer in his Phæacians, is probably not the only legend from the North Sea area which has been included by the great poet in his verses. We have already mentioned the remark of Radermacher that Homer's tale of the saving veil of Ino shows great similarity with the Nordic legend of the saving veil of a sea nymph. It is possible that here also the tale of Homer is based on an ancient Nordic legend. Other legends from the " Phæacia " can be traced back more easily to their Nordic origin, as they either betray their Nordic origin by their content or they can be found in the Nordic legends in pure and original form.

Among the legends which betray through the land of their origin their content belongs the adventure of Odysseus in the land of the Læstrygonians. Odysseus says:

> For six days we forged ahead, never lying up even at night, and on the seventh we came to Telepylus, Lamus' stronghold in the Læstrygonian land, where shepherds bringing in their flocks at night hail and are answered by their fellows driving out at dawn. For in this land nightfall and morning tread so closely on each other's heels that a man who could do without sleep might earn a double set of wages, one as a neatherd and the other for shepherding white flocks of sheep. Here we found an excellent harbour, closed in on all sides by an unbroken ring of precipitous cliffs, with two bold headlands facing each other at the mouth so as to leave only a narrow channel in between. The captains of my squadron all steered their craft straight into the cove and tied up in the sheltered waters within. They remained close together, for it was obvious that the spot was never exposed to a heavy or even a moderate sea, and the weather outside was bright and calm.*

* Penguin Classics, p. 160.

Already Crates of Malos (170 B.C.) had recognised that in these verses the short summer's night of the high North is described. Only in the North are the summer nights as light as described here. This view of Crates has been adhered to by most Homer scholars, and therefore the land of the Læstrygonians has been fixed on the Norwegian coast.

We also have to give our support to this view. We have already pointed out that in antiquity the far North was always understood by the description of districts " where day and night come near to each other and talk to each other," or " where the paths of day and night are so close that the leaving shepherd meets the homecoming shepherd."

That the North people, who after all are the source of this legend, knew the Norwegian highland is proved by the graphic description of the high mountains to the north of Atlantis which has been handed down to us in the Atlantis report. The mountains there beyond the sea were said to have been without parallel as far as height, number and beauty were concerned.

In this connection it is important to emphasise that the story of the Læstrygonians can also be found in Nordic legends. Saxo Grammaticus, who collected the Nordic legends in the twelfth century A.D., wrote down one which comes remarkably close to the Læstrygonian story. As it is difficult to assume that the Norse people read Homer during the heathen age and applied to themselves a legend which was placed by Homer in the far North, no other conclusion is left but that Homer incorporated in his poem the Læstrygonian stories from ancient Nordic legend.

### 3. THE VOYAGE TO THE CIMMERIANS

Many scholars agree that in the following verses a country in the far North is understood.

Odysseus says of his voyage to the Cimmerians:

Thus she brought us to the deep-flowing River of Ocean and the frontiers of the World, where the fog-bound Cimmerians live in the City of the Perpetual Mist. When the bright sun climbs the sky and puts the stars to flight, no ray from him can

penetrate to them, nor can he see them as he drops from
heaven and sinks once more to earth. For dreadful Night has
spread her mantle over the heads of that unhappy folk.*

There in the land of the Cimmerians, on the coast of
Oceanos, Odysseus implores the souls of the dead. Here we
are again led to the " end of Oceanos," that is, the farthest
North, where lies the Sea of the Dead, or the Island of the
Dead. Ancient commentators of the Homeric epic have
already remarked that this story takes place at the North Sea.

Most scholars have located the land of the Cimmerians
in the most northern stretches of the North Sea, because they
believe that Homer was referring to the long winter night
of the far North and its many months of darkness. Henning,
on the other hand, has pointed out that when we study
closely Homer's statements nothing is said of a " continuous
night." Homer does not describe a country where the sun
always remains below the horizon, but where the sun rises
and sets, but cannot be seen on account of the fog. In other
words, the sun cannot be seen for meteorological, and not
for astronomical, reasons. For this reason Henning is
inclined to identify the land of the Cimmerians with the
British Isles, where such fog often occurs. But Britain is not
at the " end of Oceanos," nor is she situated near the Island
of the Dead. We have therefore to identify the Cymbrian
peninsula with the land of the Cimmerians. Here was the
" end of Oceanos," here every crossing was prevented by
an enormous sea of mud, as reported in the Atlantis report,
and later by Pytheas. Here, quite near the coast, was the
Island of the Dead, the sunken royal island of the Atlanteans.
Here lived a people which since time immemorial has been
named the Cimmerians, or Cymbrians. It is quite possible
that after the great climatic catastrophes of the thirteenth
and twelfth centuries B.C. when a " new, difficult period for
the people of the North Sea areas began," marked by very
wet weather, the people of the Cymbrian peninsula were
often unable to see the sun through the fog and the clouds.

That the legend of the land of fog of the Cimmerians

* Penguin Classics, *Ibid.*, p. 175.

originates from the centuries after the catastrophe is shown by the story of the exorcism and arrival of the dead from the Island of the Dead.

This legend has also been preserved with great similarity in the North. The hero of the Nordic legend is called Thorkill; he is like Odysseus in many ways and many traits are similar in both heroes. Thorkill also travels like Odysseus across the World Ocean and reaches the coast of a country that is continually shrouded in fog and clouds. The description of the country visited by Thorkill is completely identical with the land of the Cimmerians of the *Odyssey*. Shadow-like ghosts approach Thorkill as they did Odysseus. They are the shadows of the Dead, who, as in the *Odyssey*, still carry the wounds which caused their death.

It is obvious that both legends are closely related to each other, and again there remains no other solution but to attribute both legends to the same source, which is based on the Island of the Dead legend of the North Sea area.

That the legend of the Island of the Dead, and the legends linked with it, like the escorts of the Dead and the Ships of the Dead, originate in the North, and not in the South, can be seen from the following facts:

1. With the legend of the Island of the Dead a curious discord is brought into Homer's conception of the next world. In the *Iliad* and in some verses of the *Odyssey* there prevails the notion, which is also general throughout Greece, that the dead stay in Hades, the underworld which was believed to be deep below the earth's surface. This notion is in contradiction to that of the Island, and the escorts, of the Dead. This concept appears much later in Greece and never succeeded in displacing the ancient notion of Hades.

2. In the North this concept of the Island of the Dead and the crossing thereto is not such a strange one. In the early Bronze Age boats' graves were built in the Nordic area, a clear proof of the existence of the notion of the Island of the Dead. It is strange that most of the boats' or ships' graves in the Nordic area are arranged in such a way that the bow

points to the Southern North Sea, regardless of the direction of the coast. Evidently the Ships of the Dead were to steer towards the sunken royal isle near Heligoland. This custom of the burial of ships remained in the North until the time of the Vikings, when the famous ships' tombs of Gokstat, Oseberg and Nydam were erected. The burial of the dead in ships is much older and much more developed in the North than was the case in the classic South.

From the above we can conclude that the origin of this concept and all legends connected with it must have travelled from the North towards the South, and not vice versa.

### 4. OTHER LEGENDS FROM THE NORTH USED BY HOMER

It is probable that other legends which Homer included in his verses have their origin in the North. Some of these legends presuppose shipping on the high seas of the World Ocean, which can only have been carried out during the time in question by the North people. Other legends have remained in purer and more original form in the North.

The tale of Calypso, who kept Odysseus prisoner for seven years on an island in the World Sea, presupposed shipping on the World Sea and a knowledge of that island, probably one of the Azores. This knowledge was shared by the Norse people, as prehistoric finds on the Azores indicate. That Calypso was a daughter of Atlas, the first King of Atlantis, and that she sent Odysseus at first to the Phæacians, or Atlanteans, seem to indicate that the relations of the goddess with the Phæacians were stronger than with the people of the Mediterranean. The seven-year captivity in the cave of the goddess reminds us strongly of similar legends from the North, for example, Tannhäuser.

The story of the sun bulls, which were slaughtered by Odysseus' companions against his advice and for which they were severely punished, can also be found in the *Saxo Grammaticus*. There Thorkill, who is so like Odysseus, landed on a distant coast where fat bulls, which were sacred to a god, were grazing. Thorkill warned his companions, but they were not put off, and they captured, killed and ate them in their great hunger. There follows also in the Nordic legend a terrible punishment; three of the companions chosen by ballot were to be sacrificed to the furious owner of the herd. The adventures of Odysseus on the island of Circe are also represented in Nordic legends. The adventures which Thorkill experienced in Gudmund's country correspond in almost all details to the Circean adventures of Odysseus. Like Circe, Gudmund invites the strangers into his hospitable house, and the most delicious dishes are offered to the men. As in the *Odyssey*, Thorkill warns his companions not to eat the offered food, and he himself refuses, like Odysseus, to accept anything. In both legends, however, the men eat the food and are transformed in consequence, in the Nordic legend into " mad people without memory," in the *Odyssey* into pigs. Gudmund's complaint about Thorkill's refusal of the delicious food is very reminiscent of a similar chapter in the *Odyssey*.

The legend of the Devil's cave, where two terrible rivers meet, is also reported very early by Adam of Bremen (A.D. 1075). He tells how Frisians travelled to the North Sea, where they eventually arrived at the Devil's cave, which was said to be the place of origin of high and low tide.

This legend is evidently an attempt to explain the origin of flood tides. As there are no flood tides in the Mediterranean it must originate from a sea where high and low tides are prevalent, and it was probably the North Sea. The enormous speed of the flood tides in this area can be seen from the speed of the stream near Bodo, in Southern Norway, which amounts to sixteen knots per hour—too strong for any sailing ship.

Another legend which shows great similarity between the Homeric and ancient Frisian traditions is the legend of the Cyclopes. In the Homeric as well as in the Frisian version of this legend the heroes of the tale reach on their wanderings a high island, surrounded everywhere by steep cliffs. According to both legends terrible giants live on these islands on the mountain peak. In both legends these giants tear apart and eat some of the seamen; the rest escape in their ships and are followed by the screaming giants. One of the brothers Grimm, the well-known fairy-tale experts, proved that the legend of Polyphemus, which is the base of this whole complex of legends, can be found in Norway in its original form. Also the detail of the cannibal giant closing his cave every night with a gigantic mountain rock which cannot be moved by many men can be found in the ancient Frisian legend as well as in Homer. Radermacher has shown that a number of Greek legends are closely connected with Nordic legends. He finds particularly in the legend of Hercules many details which find their counterpart in the European North.

All the scholars of our time have pointed out that Eratosthenes, the director of the famous library of Alexandria (A.D. 275), had noticed that Homer's verses were tedious fiction because they place events and legends in Western or Southern countries which in reality originated in the farthest North. Strabo attempted to clear Homer of these reproaches by devoting almost the whole first book of his world geography to justify Homer. He explains that although Homer betrays a curious knowledge of the far North in his descriptions, and even places a number of his hero's adventures there, he can thank the Cimmerians for a knowledge which was remarkable for his time.

It is possible that Strabo's assumption is correct, and that Homer owes his remarkable knowledge of Nordic conditions and legends to the Cimmerians, or North people. This question is as difficult to solve as the source of Homer's excellent knowledge of Troy, which was destroyed several hundred years before his time.

We can therefore say about the legends handed down to us by Homer that many are very ancient legends of the North which had already existed long before the Nordic people turned to Greece and Asia Minor. We have investigated these legends in this book about Atlantis, because they were in all probability once told in the homes and harbour meeting-places on Basileia, and later, after the destruction of the royal island, appeared on the coasts of the North Sea.

It is certain that not only did Homer vividly describe Holy Ilium, the royal town of the Trojans, in his Phæacia, but also Basileia, the royal town of the Atlanteans, the " Holy Isle " of the North Sea area; it can be said of him when he sings of Holy Ilium:

> You sing about everything so wonderfully
> As if you had seen or experienced it yourself

# THE REDISCOVERY OF ATLANTIS

DURING 1948 it became clear to me, after long and detailed studies, that the Atlantis report is to a large extent a reliable historical source, and Basileia, the royal isle of the Atlanteans, must be looked for six miles east of Heligoland.

In those days I entertained little hope that the North Sea would have left any visible traces of the settlements of the sunken island. But in spite of this I obtained a sea map in order to investigate whether at the spot in question there may still be the remains of a hill, or an exceptional collection of rock stones.

I shall never forget the moment when I unrolled the sea map. I saw at once, exactly at the spot in question, a hill low on every side, as well as extensive collections of stones, among them also " great stones." These stones gave the underwater hill, which arose from the flat sea bed, the name " stone ground."

I was immediately convinced that here on the bed of the sea was the final proof of the reliability of Plato's statements, and of the correctness of my theories. If it was possible to find here any remains or traces of settlement, if only an artificial arrangement of the " great stones,' then it could only be the final remains of Basileia.

Experts, of course, told me that these stones were either growing rock, or ancient moraines, but certainly not traces of human settlements. But no one had bothered to investigate the stone ground, and it remained a geological puzzle.

I obtained for myself ancient maps of Heligoland. On one map, drawn in 1649 by the greatest cartographer of his

(1) A square paving stone from Atlantis.

(2) Perforated stones—anchor stones—from Atlantis.

The gravestones over the sunken Atlantis. The northern point of Heligoland.

time, Johannes Meyer, probably based on ancient Heligoland legends and traditions, there was marked on the exact spot of the stone ground a " *templum* " and a " *castellum.*" The oldest-known map of Heligoland, dating back to 1570, indicates seven churches to the east of Heligoland, and says: " Can be seen during lowest ebb." Old Heligoland fishermen told me that on the stone ground were great stone walls, and that here was once a " golden town " which had been unbelievably wealthy.

These statements gave fresh hope that it might be possible to find remains of settlements on the stone ground. I decided to search for these remains of habitations.

A task of unusual fascination awaited me. Here was once a town mentioned by Ramses III and the priests in Sais, which was reported by Solon and Plato, the prophets Amos and Jeremiah, and which was sung by Homer in unforgettable verses. This spot had been sought for more than 2,500 years, by " fools and wise men, idealists, poets, philosophers and scientists." A sea of ink had been spilt, and mountains of paper written on and printed, in order to find this spot, the royal hill of Atlantis. And here lay, covered with ruins, the " most secret town in the history of the world."

But what difficulties there were in the way of a solution! When for the first time I showed an expert on the west coast of Schleswig-Holstein the sea map and said, " Here was Atlantis, and here I shall search for the remains of its royal castle," he laughed loudly and declared that I was a fool.

I did not know at that time the various works about the presence of brass and pure copper on Heligoland. But as the Atlantis report mentioned this, I dared to say that on Heligoland there must have been copper and brass. A prominent geologist in Germany answered that I must be a crank, because there had never been copper on Heligoland.

In order to obtain some money for the investigation of the stone ground, I began to lecture on the subject of " Atlantis in the North Sea." A newspaper article stated that the Atlantis report of Plato was a philosophical-political Utopia, and that the quoting of the *Odyssey* as a source was similar to the habit of some sects of pronouncing on all and everything from the Bible.

The anonymous writer tried to compensate for his poor knowledge of the subject with strong phrases. Another " expert " announced that he had extensive archæological proof for the origin of the North and Sea peoples in the Balkan peninsula. Another wrote that Spanuth must not think that he can solve a problem which generations of scholars have been unable to solve. In other words, a cry of protest arose before my little ship could set out on its voyage to the stone ground. Finally I was politely asked officially to give up this " nonsense " about Atlantis. But there were also favourable comments. Many well-known scholars in various branches of science supported me with valuable advice, literary sources and special research. After a lecture in Munich several people were generously prepared to finance an expedition to the stone ground.

When the voyage of reconnaissance was ready to start on July 15th, 1950, heavy storms swept across the North Sea for nine days. The funds at my disposal were sufficient for ten days. We had to lie idle in harbour until the penultimate night and listen to the hopeless sea-weather reports. Finally the weather cleared in the early hours of the tenth day. The sea calmed, the sun broke through the clouds and we could depart. When we reached the neighbourhood of the stone ground we realised that the light buoy which marked this sandbank had been driven off by the heavy storms. So we had to approach the stone ground step by step through countless soundings. At last we had found the right spot; the sounding-lead showed a depth of twenty-seven feet and we could feel the lead touching great stones. I gauged the exact distance to the dunes and the rock of Heligoland, the diver entered the water and began to report his first observations through the telephone. Then the air thundered with the roar of countless aircraft engines. An English bomber squadron used the fine weather to unload its bombs on Heligoland. Sky-high exposive clouds shot into the air and the diver had to come on board at once, as his life was endangered by the strong underwater pressure of the explosions. We had to leave the danger zone and wait. The day passed, the last bombers left, and there was nothing left but to make for home.

We approached Cuxhaven late at night. Not a single star could be seen and the lighthouse of Heligoland was extinguished. I was standing on the ship trying to forget the disappointments of the last days. Was everything which I had undertaken really nonsense, as some people had said? Was it wrong, as an eminent man had declared, to sacrifice time and money to prove the position of Atlantis? Was it not really foolish to attempt to find the ruins of Atlantis in this ocean desert? Was it not possible that I was trying to solve a problem which had been described by scholars as insoluble? Yes, it was difficult enough to find Troy, although "Holy Ilium" was on the mainland and its existence was well proven by many reports. Atlantis, however, was submerged beneath the sea, and muddy waters hid it from the searching eye. Was the critic not right who had warned me not to search for Atlantis, as the problem was much more difficult than that of Troy! For the hundredth time I weighed the arguments against my theory and scrutinised my own method of investigation. For the sake of peace, would it not be better to give up this " nonsense " about Atlantis?

All these questions worried me during that dark night. But then I thought of the fate of other outsiders in the world of science, and how they relentlessly pursued their chosen path. I told myself that all the objections, after close and careful scrutiny, can be shown to be easily refutable and to have been pronounced without deep thought. I thought with gratitude of those scholars who had advised me, and of my friends who had helped me. None of them would understand me if I gave up the problem of " Atlantis " so soon before its final solution.

When we eventually left Cuxhaven that grey, early morning the struggle of the night was finished; I had resolved not to give up my " old love " Atlantis, and to return as soon as possible.

After some days I returned on another boat to the stone ground. The weather report had forecast " light, moderate winds " in the German Bay. But when we approached a heavy storm broke loose—we had to return and seek shelter in the nearest harbour.

We had collected, however, valuable experience for the continuation of diving operations on the stone ground. I knew from the stories of the Heligoland fishermen that there were mighty stone walls and ruins on the sea bed at the stone ground, and I recognised that a research ship must use the harbour of Heligoland if the diving operations at the stone ground were to have any chance of success. It also became clear to me that on account of the weather conditions in the German Bay the time required for an expedition would be four weeks, and not ten days.

Two years later Heligoland was freed by the British, and therefore the use of the harbour became possible.

In November 1950 I was invited to give a lecture on Atlantis in an eminent club in London. After the lecture the president of the club rose and said: " Never have I approached a lecture with so much scepticism, and never have I been so convinced of the correctness of the course of investigation than by your lecture. How can we help? "

In this way a new expedition was made possible in the summer of 1952, after Heligoland's return to German territory.

Again there was a heavy storm when we approached Heligoland on July 15th. This time we had to wait fourteen, not ten days before the storms subsided. When we finally started the crossing to Heligoland in our little ship there was a slight breeze. When we entered Heligoland harbour a heavy storm broke out during the night, and the waves broke over the breakwaters. Only on July 31st could we begin to undertake the first diving attempts on the stone ground. I calculated that it would take us forty-three minutes to cover the distance to the stone ground. Exactly to the minute the ship stopped, the anchor was thrown overboard—here must be the ruins of the royal castle of Atlantis! The diver entered the water.

I was connected with him by telephone, and anxiously waited for his news. After only a few minutes he said: "I can see in front of me a high stone wall! I am approaching it. At the foot of the wall are gigantic stones. I am measuring one stone, it is six feet long and three feet wide. There are similar stones to the right; many of them are square. I shall try and climb the wall—it is at least six feet high and consists of big stones—now I am on top. I can recognise a second wall, parallel to that I am standing on. I am walking along the top of the first wall."

After a little while the diver reported again: " This is the end of the wall, it looks like a crater in the wall. I descend. At the foot of the wall towards the crater there is a particularly big stone, six feet long and three feet wide. In the bottom of the crater there is white sand, only small stones. Now I can see the continuation of the wall on the other side of the crater." The " crater " had evidently been a gap in the walls. The diver continued: " I now climb the other side of the wall, and parallel to this I can see the second wall. Between the two parallel walls there is white sand. I am now walking in the trench between the walls. I climb the parallel wall. It has the same structure as the first. I am now walking along the top of the wall. I can see now for the first time white stones, quite large; until now I have only seen red stones. I cannot see the end of either wall! Now I can see white stones again, arranged side by side, and above them red stones."

We had similar information during the following days when diving was possible. Once the diver found a spot at which in the interior of the wall structure a stone wall branched off at right angles. The walls were measured, and they were thirty-six feet in width, and six to eight feet in height. According to our measurements, which correspond to the statements of the Heligoland fishermen, the wall structures stretched to a length of about half a mile. The width of the total structure measured seven hundred and fifty to nine hundred feet.

The diver declared after his diving operations: " It is impossible that these walls, which are so symmetrical and parallel, could have been formed by natural means, and I have no doubt that they were erected by human hands."

During calm seas it was possible to make out the whole wall ramparts from sea level. The strong tidal current breaks at the walls, which arise from a depth of twenty-two feet and therefore act as underwater breakwaters. Tidal limits are thereby created on the surface and a smooth level sea is formed.

The fishermen on Heligoland know precisely the wall ramparts on the stone ground. They catch their finest lobsters in the great stones at the foot of the walls and they often have three hundred to four hundred lobster baskets along the walls of the stone ground. As every lobster basket is marked on the surface by a flag buoy, it is easy to recognise the size and shape of the structure by the position of the flag buoys.

The fishermen have been handed down by their ancestors the legend that these walls on the stone ground are the remains of a " golden town " which sank here in prehistoric times.

At the end of the diving operations we were convinced that the discovered ramparts were in fact the " bulwark " which, according to the Atlantis report and the *Odyssey*, surrounded the royal castle and the temple. Between the statements of the Atlantis report on the one hand, and the conditions which were found there on the other, there is complete agreement.

1. The wall ramparts were in fact six miles from the mainland, on a hill which was low on all sides.

2. The wall ramparts were in fact five hundred feet long, and surrounded the structures on the top of the hill.

3. The wall ramparts were in fact made of " stone, partly white, red and black "; they had " gaps " and gates, as recorded in the Atlantis report.

4. In these parts there had really been orichalc, or amber. We found a large piece in the area of the stone ground, and the fishermen who throw their nets there often find amber. The amber which is washed ashore on the nearby coast

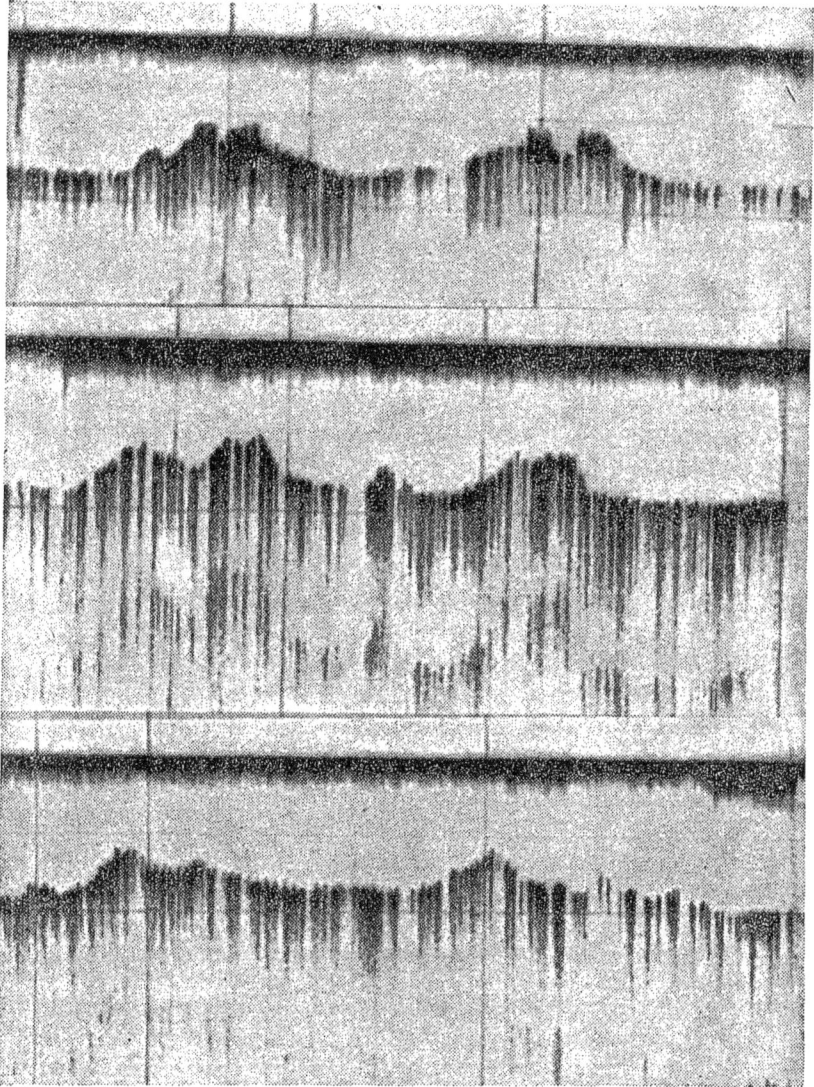

Echograms of the ramparts (1) and the ruins (2 and 3) in the " Stone-ground " off Heligoland. Shortly after distinguishing the various objects, the ship returned over them. The right half of the picture, therefore, is a mirror image of the object in the left half, only some 30 metres farther north.

also originates from this sunken island, where it must have once been found in many places.

5. There is also on the nearby rock of Heligoland " copper in pure and melted form." According to the legend, there were even canals and watercourses made of copper.

6. The ancient tradition, which has been recorded in the legends and old maps of Heligoland, reports a temple and a castle which were situated on the hill of the stone ground. The god which was worshipped here was called *Fosites*, which in all probability is *Posides*, as Poseidon was called in ancient Dorian, whose main sanctuary, according to the Atlantis report, was situated on Basileia. " Fosites land," therefore, the name for the sunken island in the ancient Frisian tradition, is the " Poseidon land " of the Atlantis report. The term " Basileia " for this island was still known by Pytheas, Diodorus of Sicily and other writers of antiquity. The term " Holy Isle," which is recorded in the Atlantis report, still remains to this day in the name " Heligoland," " Holy Land," *terra sancta.*

We had therefore found the royal island of the Atlantean, or Teutonic, kingdom, and the mystery of the " most mysterious town in the history of the world " has been solved.

.   .   .   .   .

Again it was night, as two years ago when we travelled home from Heligoland. But on this occasion countless stars were shining above us, and the lighthouse of Heligoland showed us the way over the stone ground to the coast.

Our ship was ploughing a silver path through the dark waves, and the sea around us was wonderfully lit. Again as I was standing at the bow, thinking of the long way which I had come since that hour. I saw in spirit the mighty and wealthy town over whose ruins our ship was passing. I thought of the people who once lived here and of that day, " full of frightful terrors," when this island was swallowed up by the North Sea, the murderous sea. Here, according to Homer's description, Odysseus once experienced splendid hospitality after his ten years of wanderings. From here he once undertook his journey home, just as we were doing ourselves, and Nausicaa bade him farewell with the words: " Farewell, Oh guest, and do not forget me when you are at home again! "

During those hours, when we travelled home across the night sea, I also thought what the Holy Script said of this island. Particularly the words of Amos went through my head: " Thus spoke the Lord, Did I not lead the Israelites out of Egypt and the Philistines out of Caphtor? "

Not " greed and terrible lust for power," as the priests in Sais once said to Solon, drove these people to undertake the " Great Migration." No, according to the words of the Bible, the Lord Himself led these people with His mighty hand during the time of the terrible natural catastrophes through a destroyed and hungry Europe into those lands where they found a new homeland and with the heritage of their old homeland created a new culture. Those events may have destroyed the ancient world, but they also created the basis for a new world, and they were the birth pangs of Western Culture.

In July and August a new expedition set out for the stone ground. On this occasion several people from Munich, who had already helped me in 1949, very kindly gave me invaluable assistance, and some firms from Southern and Northern Germany put at my disposal the necessary means and equipment. This year also the weather was not very favourable; only for eight of the thirty days was it possible for the diver to search the stone ground. Apart from air-tube equipment we were able to work with a new air pressure machine which proved most satisfactory. With this apparatus the diver was able to swim freely immediately above the sea bed. The diver, Mr. Fries, was able to undertake twenty-seven diving journeys on the stone ground; whilst I myself repeatedly dived with this apparatus and saw the remaining ruins.

Visibility was very poor on account of countless diatoms which floated in the water. It looked as if we were standing in a blizzard in front of a dark rock wall. This muddy water unfortunately made underwater photography impossible.

It was, however, possible for the diver to make the following observations:

1. At the southern part of the stone ground there is a wall section, the base of which lies forty feet below, and at an angle of forty-five degrees. The top of the wall is about three feet wide. The wall consists of round stones of the size of a pumpkin, evenly packed and closely wedged together. Flint plates of about four to six feet in size lie irregularly at the foot of the wall, and some also on the wall proper. These plates are even on both sides and have rectangular corners in relation to the surface.

This rampart was found by me at different places in a northerly direction, as well as a second parallel wall of a similar kind.

2. In front of the southern section of the wall I found at different places under layers of rubble, i.e. round stones of the size of a head, horizontally-lying flint plates which were fixed to each other. According to my opinion, these stones could not have been arranged so evenly by Nature, as these horizontally-lying plates could only be found under the layer of rubble.

At the places, where there was no deposit of rubble, these flat, evenly strong flint plates of different sizes were lying in the sand. It appeared as if the plates, which were covered by the rubble, were only kept in their horizontal position by the rubble which had fallen on them, whilst the other plates had been thrown about in a disorderly fashion by the action of the sea.

These plate covers were also found by me at different places within the ramparts. Several specimens from the rampart were brought on board. Investigations showed that they were without exception flint plates, in contrast to the round stones, which consisted solely of granite or similar stone.

3. In the same area, a hundred and fifty feet south of the surrounding ramparts, I found between the plates and other stones half a tube rising out of the sand; this was brought on board. At the same spot I saw during later divings a larger,

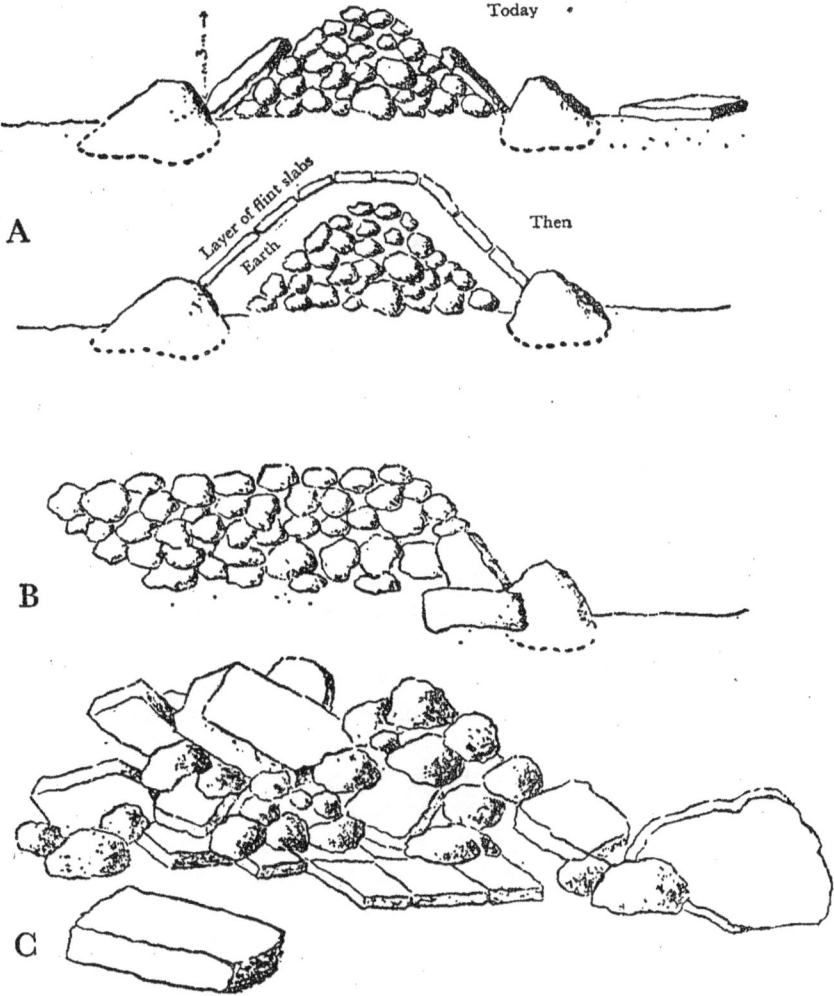

Sketches drawn by the diver, Eberhard Fries, of the stone wall and the ruins discovered by him in the " Stoneground." (A) The stone wall today and a reconstruction of it in the past; (B) The beginning of the wall at the gateway (side view); (C) Fallen ruins covering a paved floor.

round stone with a hole in the middle which was also brought aboard. There I also found a larger flint stone with an unusual appearance. Within the ramparts, about six hundred feet north of the southern tip, I found under the rubble a horizontal plane which consisted of evenly strong plates of about fifteen to twenty inches width. These plates were closely joined together. The surfaces of these plates were completely smooth and even. The ground under these plates consisted of sand or chalk clay, and there was no rubble below it. One of these plates I brought on board. The other plates could not be brought aboard on account of the strong tide which had just begun. Whether the plate cover continued under the rubble I was unable to determine, as the shifting of the other rubble heaps proved impossible. The strong tide which began prevented further work.

4. To the north of the stone ground I found, amongst others, a stone with a circular hole which was also brought on board.

The total impression which remained after the investigation of the ramparts and the planes within the rampart was that we had here traces of human settlement groups. A natural formation of the regularly arranged ramparts and the regularly lying horizontal plate surfaces must be looked upon as impossible.

As a member of the Club Alpin Sous-Marin I have undertaken in the Mediterranean, in the Baltic and North Seas, and in many lakes of Europe several hundred diving expeditions, reaching depths down to a hundred and twenty-five feet. Nowhere to date have I found similar formations.

These remarks of the diver, Mr. Fries, are a valuable addition to the observations of the stone ground which Mr. Belte had already undertaken in 1952. It was very important for the success of our expedition in 1953 that we could gain an insight into the echographic registrations which were made by the survey ship *Atair* over the stone ground. The diver Bendeg of the survey ship *Wega* found at the same time a street covered with cobblestones which he followed for a hundred and fifty feet.

We now have five divers who have seen the stone ground: Belte, Fries, Mrs. Fries, Bendeg and myself. All agree that the ramparts, rampart gaps, cobbled streets and the places covered with tiles were not formed by natural means, but must surely have been created by the hands of men.

## EPILOGUE

IN the preface we compared the Atlantis report with a treasure chamber which makes it possible for us to ascertain valuable scientific knowledge and astonishing insight into the habits, beliefs, ideas, struggles and sufferings of our ancestors who lived more than three thousand years ago, and it explains many puzzles of our history.

When we glance back at the results of our investigations we are able to confirm this assertion.

Through the Atlantis report one of the most important epochs of the history of the West was made clearer which up till now was shrouded in mystery and resisted every attempt of comprehension. We saw that the gigantic regroupings of population were caused during the last third of the thirteenth century B.C. by world-wide natural catastrophes, when a mighty wave of people overflowed through Europe and Asia Minor into Egypt, destroying many old cultures, but at the same time laying the foundations for a new world, that of the classic and therefore the Western world. The orientalising of the South-East area, which was progressing uninterruptedly until the invasion of the North people, came to an abrupt ending, and, above all, Greece, which had appeared to be completely lost for Europe, was taken away from the Orient. In the following centuries Greece developed more and more into a centre of Western culture. The dead material which was found was given life through the Atlantis report, and many questions were answered which hitherto appeared insoluble.

The Atlantis report has also made it possible for us to prove that the North people of Ramses III, the Philistines of the Old Testament, the Atlanteans of Plato and the Phæacians of Homer were one and the same. Several ancient sources were thereby opened up which gave us reliable information about the habits, beliefs and ideas, struggles and sufferings of our ancestors more than three thousand years ago. In this way a race was brought nearer to us, and was filled with new life, a race which scholars of prehistory had previously always described as " greatly puzzling," a race which so far we had only known by its archæological remains, and not by written reports and contemporary pictures.

The hitherto inexplicable decline of the high culture and impressive power of the North Sea people at the end of the Bronze Age has now been explained, and we have shown that the migration to the South of the Norse people did not happen during the height of their power, but during a time of extreme peril.

The hitherto hotly debated and never answered question about the original home of the Greeks, and that of the related Philistines, has been solved, and the last causes of the puzzling relationship between the early Greeks and the races of the North Sea area have been made clear.

The Atlantis report helped to throw light on many other problems. It will surely help to solve many other riddles, if we can only trust the love of truth of the great Plato and take to heart his reminder:

Truth must be searched for with the whole heart!

# THE LEGEND OF ATLANTIS

AS already mentioned, Plato has left us the Atlantis legend in two different places of his writings: the *Dialogues* of Timæus and Critias. In the *Dialogues* of Timæus, the older of the two, we hear that some friends of the wise Socrates gathered in his presence, and the following is an extract of their discourse:

*Critias:* I will tell an old-world story which I heard from an aged man; for Critias (the Older) was, as he said, at that time nearly ninety years of age, and I was about ten years of age. Now the day was that day of the Apaturia which is called the registration of youth, at which, according to custom, our parents gave prizes for recitations, and the poems of several poets were recited by us boys, and many of us sang the poems of Solon, which were new at the time. One of our tribe, either because this was his real opinion, or because he thought that he would please Critias, said that in his judgment Solon was not only the wisest of men, but also the noblest of poets. The old man, as I well remember, brightened up at this and said, smiling: Yes, Amynander, if Solon had only, like other poets, made poetry the business of his life, and had completed the tale which he brought with him from Egypt, and had not been compelled, by reason of the factions and troubles, which he found stirring in this country when he came home, to attend to other matters, in my opinion he would have been as famous as Homer or Hesiod, or any poet.

And what was the poem about, Critias? said the person who addressed him.

About the greatest action which the Athenians ever did, and which ought to have been the most famous, but which, through the lapse of time and the destruction of the actors, has not come down to us.

Tell us, said the other, the whole story, and how and from whom Solon heard this veritable tradition.

He replied: At the head of the Egyptian Delta, where the River Nile divides, there is a certain district which is called the district of Sais, and the great city of the district is also called Sais, and is the city from which Amasis the king was sprung. And the citizens have a deity who is their foundress; she is called in the Egyptian tongue Neith, and is asserted by them to be the same whom the Hellenes called Athene. Now the citizens of this city are great lovers of the Athenians, and say that they are in some way related to them. Thither came Solon, who was received by them with great honour; and he asked the priests, who were most skilful in such matters, about antiquity, and made the discovery that neither he nor any other Hellene knew anything worth mentioning about the times of old. On one occasion, when he was drawing them on to speak of antiquity, he began to tell about the most ancient things in our part of the world—about Phoroneus, who is called " the first," and about Niobe; and after the Deluge, to tell of the lives of Deucalion and Pyrrha; and he traced the genealogy of their descendants, and attempted to reckon how many years old were the events of which he was speaking, and to give the dates. Thereupon, one of the priests, who was of a very great age, said: O Solon, Solon, you Hellenes are but children, and there is never an old man who is an Hellene. Solon hearing this, said, What do you mean? I mean to say, he replied, that in mind you are all young; there is no old opinion handed down among you by ancient tradition, nor any science which is hoary with age. And I will tell you the reason of this. There have been, and will be again, many destructions of mankind arising out of many causes; the greatest have been brought about by the agencies of fire and water, and other lesser ones by innumerable other causes. There is a story, which even you have preserved, that once upon a time Phaëtön, the son of Helios, having yoked the steeds in his father's chariot, because he was not able to drive them in the path of his father, burnt up all that was upon the earth, and was himself destroyed by a thunderbolt. Now, this has the form of a myth, but really signifies a declination of the bodies moving around the earth and in the heavens, and a great conflagration of things upon the earth recurring at long intervals of time; when this happens, those who

13—A

live upon the mountains and in dry and lofty places are more liable to destructions than those who dwell by rivers or on the seashore. And from this calamity the Nile, who is our never failing saviour, saves and delivers us. When, on the other hand, the gods purge the earth with a deluge of water, among you, herdsmen and shepherds on the mountains are the survivors, whereas those of you who live in cities are carried by the rivers into the sea. But in this country, neither at that time nor at any other, does the water come from above on the fields, having always a tendency to come up from below, for which reason the things preserved here are said to be the oldest. The fact is, that wherever the extremity of winter frost or of summer sun does not prevent, the human race is always increasing at times, and at other times diminishing in numbers. And whatever happened either in your country or in ours, or in any other region of which we are informed—if any action which is noble or great or in other way remarkable has taken place, all that has been written down of old, and is preserved in our temples; whereas you and other nations are just being provided with letters and the other things which states require; and then, at the usual period, the stream from heaven descends like a pestilence, and leaves only those of you who are destitute of letters and education; and thus have to begin all over again as children, and know nothing of what happened in ancient times, either among us or among yourselves. As for those genealogies of yours which you have recounted to us, Solon, they are no better than the tales of children; for in the first place you remember one deluge only, whereas there were many of them; and in the next place, you do not know that there dwelt in your land the fairest and noblest race of men which ever lived, of whom you and your whole city are but a seed or remnant. And this was unknown to you, because for many generations the survivors of that destruction died and made no sign. For there was a time, Solon, before the great deluge of all, when the city, which now is Athens, was first in war and was pre-eminent for the excellence of her laws, and is said to have performed the noblest deeds and to have had the fairest constitution of any of which tradition tells, under the face of heaven. Solon marvelled at this, and earnestly requested the priest to inform him exactly and in order about these former citizens. You are welcome to hear about them, Solon, said the priest, both for your own sake and for that of the city, and above all, for the sake of the goddess who is the common patron and protector and educator of both our cities. She founded your city a thousand years before ours, receiving from the Earth and Hephæstus the seed of your race, and then she founded ours, the constitution of which is set down in our sacred registers as eight thousand years old. As touching the citizens of nine thousand years ago, I will briefly inform you of their laws and of the noblest of their actions; and the exact particulars of the whole we will hereafter go through at our leisure in the sacred registers themselves. If you compare these very laws with your own you will find that many of ours are the counterpart of ours as they were in the olden time. In the first place, there is the caste of priests, which is separated from all the others; next there are the artificers, who exercise their several crafts by themselves and without admixture of any other; and also there is the class of shepherds and that of hunters, as well as that of husbandmen; and you will observe, too, that the warriors in Egypt are separated from all the other classes, and are commanded by the law to engage in war; moreover, the weapons with which they are equipped are shields and spears, and this the goddess taught first among you, and then in Asiatic countries, and we among the Asiatics first adopted. Then as to wisdom, do you observe what care the law took from the very first, searching out and comprehending the whole order of things down to prohecy and medicine (the latter with a view to health); and out of these divine elements drawing what was needed for human life, and adding every sort of knowledge which was connected with them. All this order and arrangement the goddess first imparted to you when establishing your city; and she chose the spot of earth in which you were born, because she saw the happy temperament of the seasons in that land would produce the wisest of men. Wherefore the goddess who was a lover both of war and of wisdom, selected and first of all settled that spot which was the most likely to produce men likest herself. And there you dwelt, having such laws as these and still better ones, and excelled all mankind in all virtue as became the children and disciples of the gods.

Many great and wonderful deeds are recorded of your state in our histories. But one of them exceeds all the rest in greatness and valour. For these histories tell of a mighty power which was aggressing wantonly against the whole of Europe and Asia, and to which your city put an end. This power came forth out of the Atlantic Ocean, for in those days the Atlantic was navigable;

and there was an island situated in front of the straits which you call the columns of Hercules; the island was larger than Libya and Asia put together, and was the way to other islands, and from the islands you might pass to the whole of the opposite continent which surrounded the true ocean; for this sea which is within the Straits of Hercules is only a harbour, having a narrow entrance, but that other is a real sea, and the surrounding land may be most truly called a continent. Now in this island of Atlantis there was a great and wonderful empire which had rule over the whole island and several others, as well as over parts of the continent, and, besides these, they subjected the parts of Libya within the columns of Hercules as far as Egypt, and of Europe as far as Tyrrhenia. The vast power thus gathered into one, endeavoured to subdue at one blow our country and yours and the whole of the land which was within the straits; and then, Solon, your country shone forth, in the excellence of her virtue and strength, among all mankind; for she was the first in courage and military skill, and was the leader of the Hellenes. And when the rest fell off from her, being compelled to stand alone, after having undergone the very extremity of danger, she defeated and triumphed over the invaders, and preserved from slavery those who were not subjected, and freely liberated all the others who dwell within the limits of Hercules. But afterwards there occurred violent earthquakes and floods; and in a single day and night of rain all your warlike men in a body sank into the earth, and the island of Atlantis in like manner disappeared, and was sunk beneath the sea. And that is the reason why the sea in those parts is impassable and impenetrable, because there is such a quantity of shallow mud in the way; and this was caused by the subsidence of the island.

I have told you shortly, Socrates, the tradition which the aged Critias heard from Solon. And when you were speaking yesterday about your city and citizens, this very tale which I am telling you came into my mind, and I could not help remarking how, by some coincidence not to be explained, you agreed in almost every particular with the account of Solon; but I did not like to speak at the moment. For as long a time had elapsed, I had forgotten too much, and I thought that I had better first of all run over the narrative in my own mind and then I would speak. And for this reason I readily assented to your request yesterday, considering that I was pretty well furnished with a theme such as the audience would approve, and to find this is in all such cases the chief difficulty.

And therefore, as Hermocrates told you, on my way home yesterday I imparted my recollections to my friends in order to refresh my memory, and during the night I thought about the words and nearly recovered them all. Truly, as is often said, the lessons which we have learned as children, make a wonderful impression on our memories, for I am not sure that I could remember all that I heard yesterday, but I should be much surprised if I forgot any of these things which I have heard very long ago. I listened to the old man telling them, when a child, with great interest at the time; he was very ready to teach me and I asked him about them a great many times, so that they were branded into my mind in ineffaceable letters. As soon as the day broke I began to repeat them to my companions, that they as well as myself might have a material of discourse. And now, Socrates, I am ready to tell you the whole tale of which this is the introduction. I will give you not only the general heads, but the details exactly as I heard them. And as to the city and citizens, which you yesterday described to us in fiction, let us transfer them to the world of reality; this shall be our city, and we will suppose that the citizens of your republic are these ancient Athenians. Let us distribute the discussion amongst us, and all endeavours as far as we can carry out your instructions. Consider then, Socrates, if this narrative is suited to the purpose, or whether we should seek for some other instead.

## 2. THE REPORT FROM THE DIALOGUE OF CRITIAS

Again some of Socrates' friends had gathered around him, and during the course of the discussion Critias said the following:

Let me begin by observing, first of all, that nine thousand was the sum of years which had elapsed since the war which was said to have taken place between all those who dwelt outside the pillars of Hercules and those who dwelt within them; this war I am now to describe. Of the combatants on the one side, the city of Athens was reported to have been the ruler and to have directed the contest; the combatants on the other side were led by the kings of the island of Atlantis, which, as I was saying, once had an extent greater than that of Libya and Asia; and when

afterwards sunk by an earthquake became an impassable barrier
of mud to voyagers sailing from hence to the ocean. The progress
of the history will unfold the various tribes of barbarians and
Hellenes which then existed, as they successively appear on the
scene; but I must begin by describing first of all the Athenians,
as they were in that day, and their enemies who fought them; and
I shall have to tell of the power and form of government of both
of them. Let us give the precedence to Athens. . . .

After describing the political constitution of Athens the
report continues as follows:

Also about the country the Egyptian priests said what is not
only probable but also true, that the boundaries were fixed by
the Isthmus, and that in the other direction they extended as
far as the heights of Cithæron and Parnes; the boundary line
came down towards the plain, having the district of Oropus on
the right, and the River Asopus on the left, as the limit towards
the sea. The land was the best in the world, and for this reason
was able in those days to support a vast army, raised from the
surrounding people. And a great proof of this fertility is, that the
part which still remains may compare with any in the world for
the variety and excellence of its fruits and the suitableness of its
pastures to every sort of animal; and besides beauty the land had
also plenty. How am I to prove this? and of what remnant of
the land then in existence may this be truly said? I would have
you observe the present aspect of the country, which is only a
promontory extending far into the sea away from the rest of the
continent, and the surrounding basin of the sea is everywhere
deep in the neighbourhood of the shore. Many great deluges
have taken place during the nine thousand years, for that is the
number of years which have elapsed since the time of which I
am speaking; and in all the ages and changes of things there has
never been any settlement of the earth flowing down the
mountains as in other places, which is worth speaking of; it has
always been carried round in a circle and disappeared in the
depths below. The consequence is, that in comparison of what
then was, there are remaining in small islets only the bones of the
wasted body, as they may be called; all the richer and softer parts
of the soil having fallen away, and the mere skeleton of the
country being left. But in former days, and in the primitive state
of the country, what are now mountains were only regarded as
hills; and the plains, as they are now termed, of Phelleus were full

of rich earth, and there was abundance of wood in the mountains. Of this last the traces still remain, for there are some of the mountains which now only afford sustenance to bees, whereas not long ago there were still remaining roofs cut from the trees growing there, which were of a size sufficient to cover the largest houses; and there were many other high trees, bearing fruit and abundance of food for cattle. Moreover, the land enjoyed rain from heaven year by year, not, as now, losing water which flows off the earth into the sea, but having an abundance in all places, and receiving and treasuring up in the close clay soil the water which drained from the heights, and letting this off into the hollows, providing everywhere abundant streams of fountains and rivers; and there may still be observed indications of them in ancient sacred places, where there are fountains; and this proves the truth of what I am saying.

Such was the natural state of the country, which was cultivated, as we may well believe, by true husbandmen, who were lovers of honour, and of a noble nature, and did the work of husbandmen, and had a soil the best in the world, and abundance of water, and in the heaven above an excellently tempered climate. . . . And next, if I have not forgotten what I heard when I was a child, I will impart to you the character and origin of their adversaries For friends should not keep their stories to themselves, but have them in common. Yet, before proceeding further in the narrative, I ought to warn you, that you must not be surprised if you should hear Hellenic names given to foreigners. I will tell you the reason of this: Solon, who was intending to use the tale for his poem, made an investigation into the meaning of the names, and found that the early Egyptians in writing them down had translated them into their own language, and he recovered the meaning of the several names and re-translated them, and copied them out again in our language. My great-grandfather, Dropidas, had the original writing, which is still in my possession, and was carefully studied by me when I was a child. Therefore, if you hear names such as are used in this country, you must not be surprised, for I have told you the reason of them. The tale, which is of great length, began as follows:

I have before remarked in speaking of the allotments of the gods, that they distributed the whole earth into portions differing in extent, and made themselves temples and sacrifices. And Poseidon, receiving for his lot the island of Atlantis, begat children by a mortal woman, and settled them in a part of the island, which I will proceed to describe. On the side towards the sea in the centre of the whole island, there was a plain which is said to have been the fairest of all plains and very fertile. Near the plain again, and also in the centre of the island at a distance of about fifty stadia, there was a mountain not very high on any side. In this mountain there dwelt one of the earth-born primeval men of that country, whose name was Evenor, and he had a wife named Leucippe, and they had an only daughter who was called Cleito. The maiden was growing up to womanhood, when her father and mother died; Poseidon fell in love with her and had intercourse with her, and breaking the ground, inclosed the hill in which she dwelt all round, making alternate zones of sea and land larger and smaller, encircling one another; there were two of land and three of water, which he turned as with a lathe, out of the centre of the island, equidistant every way, so that no man could get to the island, for ships and voyages were not as yet heard of. He himself, as he was a god, found no difficulty in making special arrangements for the centre island, bringing two streams of water under the earth, which he caused to ascend as springs, one of warm water and the other of cold, and making every variety of food to spring up abundantly in the earth. He also begat and brought up five pairs of male children, dividing the island of Atlantis into ten portions; he gave the first-born of the eldest pair his mother's dwelling and the surrounding allotment, which was the largest and best, and made him king over the rest; the others he made princes, and gave them rule over many men, and a large territory. And he named them all; the eldest, who was the king, he named Atlas, and from him the whole island and the ocean received the name of Atlantic. To his twin brother, who was born after him, and obtained as his lot the extremity of the island towards the pillars of Hercules, as far as the country which is still called the region of Gades in that part of the world, he gave the name which in the Hellenic language is Eumelus, in the language of the country which is named after him, Gadeirus. Of the second pair of twins he called one Ampheres, and the other Evæmon. To the third pair of twins he gave the name Mneseus to the elder, and Autochton to the one who followed him. Of the fourth pair of twins he called the elder Elasippus, and the younger Mestor. And of the fifth pair he gave to the elder the name of Azæs, and to the younger that of Diaprepes. All these and their descendants were the inhabitants and rulers of divers islands in the open sea; and also, as has been already said, they held sway in the other direction over the country within the pillars as far as Egypt and Tyrrhenia. Now Atlas had a numerous and honourable family, and his eldest branch always retained the kingdom which the eldest son handed on to his eldest for many generations; and they had such an amount of wealth as was never before possessed by kings and potentates, and is not likely ever to be again, and they were furnished with everything which they could have, both in the city and country. For because of the greatness of their empire many things were brought to them from foreign countries, and the island itself provided much of what was required by them for the uses of life. In the first place, they dug out of the earth whatever was to be found there, mineral as well as metal, and that which is now only a name, orichalcum, was dug out of the earth in many parts of the island, and with the exception of gold was esteemed the most precious of metals among the men of those days. There was an abundance of wood for carpenter's work, and sufficient maintenance for tame and wild animals. Moreover, there were a great number of elephants in the island, and there was provision for animals of every kind, both for those which live in lakes and marshes and rivers, and also for those which live in mountains and plains, and therefore for the animal which is the largest and most voracious of them. Also whatever fragrant things there are in the earth, whether roots, or herbage, or woods, or distilling drops of flowers or fruits, grew and thrived in that land; and again, the cultivated fruit of the earth, both the dry edible fruit and other species of food, which we call by the general name of legumes, and the fruits having a hard rind, affording drinks and meats and ointments, and good store of chestnuts and the like, which may be used to play with, and are fruits which spoil with keeping, and the pleasant kind of dessert, which console us after dinner, when we are full and tired of eating—all these that sacred island lying beneath the sun, brought forth fair and wondrous in infinite abundance. All these things they received from the earth, and they employed themselves in constructing their temples and palaces and harbours and docks; and they arranged the whole country in the following manner:

First of all they bridged over the zones of sea which surrounded the ancient metropolis, and made a passage into and out of the royal palace; and then they began to build the palace in the habitation of the god and of their ancestors. This they continued to ornament in successive generations, every king surpassing the one who came before him to the utmost of his power, until they made the building a marvel to behold for size and beauty. And beginning from the sea they dug a canal of three hundred feet in width and nine hundred feet in depth, and fifty stadia in length, which they carried through to the outermost zone, making a passage from the sea up to this, which became a harbour, and leaving an opening sufficient to enable the largest vessels to find ingress. Moreover, they divided the zones of land which parted the zones of sea, constructing bridges of such a width as would leave a passage for a single trireme to pass out of one into another, and roofed them over; and there was a way underneath for the ships; for the banks of the zones were raised considerably above the water. Now the largest of the zones into which a passage was cut from the sea was three stadia in breadth, and the zone of land which came next of equal breadth; but the next two, as well as the zone of water as of land, were two stadia, and the one which surrounded the central island was a stadium only in width. The island in which the palace was situated had a diameter of five stadia. This and the zones and the bridge, which was the sixth part of a stadium in width, they surrounded by a stone wall, on either side placing towers, and gates on the bridges where the sea passed in. The stone which was used in the work they quarried from underneath the centre island, and from underneath the zones, on the outer as well as the inner side. One kind of stone was white, another black, and a third red, and as they quarried they at the same time hollowed out docks double within, having roofs formed out of the native rock. Some of their buildings were simple, but in others they put together different stones which they intermingled for the sake of ornament, to be a natural source of delight. The entire circuit of the wall, which went round the outermost one, they covered with a coating of brass, and the circuit of the next wall they coated with tin, and the third, which encompassed the citadel, flashed with the red light of orichalcum. The palaces in the interior of the citadel were constructed in this manner: In the centre was a holy temple dedicated to Cleito and Poseidon, which remained inaccessible, and was surrounded by an enclosure of gold; this was the spot in which they originally begat the race of the princes, and thither they annually brought the fruits of the earth in their season from all the ten portions, and performed sacrifices to each of them. Here, too, was Poseidon's own temple of a stadium in length, and half a stadium in width, and of a proportionate height, having a sort of barbaric splendour. All the outside of the temple, with the exception of the pinnacles, they covered with silver and orichalcum; all the other parts of the walls and pillars and floor they lined with orichalcum. In the temple they placed statues of gold—the charioteer of six winged horses—and of such a size that he touch the roof of the buildings with his head; around him there were a hundred Nereids riding on dolphins, for such was thought to be the number of them in that day. There were also in the interior of the temple other images which had been dedicated by private individuals. And around the temple on the outside were placed statues of gold of all the ten kings and of their wives, and there were many other great offerings both of kings and of private individuals, coming both from the city itself and the foreign cities over which they held sway. There was an altar too, which in size and workmanship corresponded to the rest of the work, and there were palaces, in like manner, which answered to the greatness of the kingdom, and the glory of the temple.

In the next place, they used fountains both of cold and hot springs; these were very abundant, and both kinds wonderfully adapted to use by reason of the sweetness and excellence of their waters. They constructed buildings about them and planted suitable trees; also cisterns, some open to the heaven, others which they roofed over, to be used in winter as warm baths; there were the king's baths, and the baths of private persons, which were kept apart; also separate baths for women, and others again for horses and cattle, and to each of them they gave as much adornment as was suitable for them. The water which ran off they carried, some to the grove of Poseidon, where were growing all manner of trees of wonderful height and beauty, owing to the excellence of the soil; the remainder was conveyed by aqueducts which passed over the bridges to the outer circles; and there were many temples built and dedicated to many gods; also gardens and places of exercise, some for men, and some set apart for horses, in both of the two islands formed by the zones; and in the centre of the larger of the two there was a racecourse of a stadium in width, and in length allowed to extend all round the island, for horses to race in. Also there were guard-horses at intervals for the bodyguard, the more trusted of whom had their duties appointed to them in the lesser zone, which was nearer the Acropolis; while the most trusted of all had houses given them within the citadel, and about the persons of the kings. The docks were full of triremes and naval stores, and all things were quite

ready for use. Enough of the plan of the royal palace. Crossing
the outer harbours, which were three in number, you would
come to a wall which began at the sea and went all round; this
was everywhere distant fifty stadia from the largest zone and
harbour, and enclosed the whole, meeting at the mouth of the
channel towards the sea. The entire area was densely crowded
with habitations; and the canal and the largest of the harbours
were full of vessels and merchants coming from all parts, who,
from their numbers, kept up a multitudinous sound of human
voices and din of all sorts night and day.

I have repeated his description of the city and the parts about
the ancient palace nearly as he gave them, and now I must
endeavour to describe the nature and arrangement of the rest of
the country. The whole country was described as being very
lofty and precipitous on the side of the sea, but the country
immediately about and surrounding the city was a level plain,
itself surrounded by mountains which descended towards the sea;
it was smooth and even, but of an oblong shape, extending in one
direction three thousand stadia, and going up the country from
the sea, through the centre of the island, two thousand stadia;
the whole region of the island lies towards the south, and is
sheltered from the north. The surrounding mountains he celebrated for their number and size and beauty, in which they
exceeded all that are now to be seen anywhere; having in them
also many wealthy inhabited villages, and rivers, and lakes, and
meadows supplying food enough for every animal, wild or tame,
and wool of various sorts, abundant for every kind of work.

I will now describe the plain, which had been cultivated
during many ages by many generations of kings. It was rectangular, and for the most part straight and oblong; and what
it wanted of the straight line followed the line of the circular
ditch. The depth, and width, and length of this ditch were
incredible, and gave the impression that such a work, in addition
to so many other works, could hardly have been wrought by the
hand of man. But I must say what I have heard. It was excavated
to the depth of a hundred feet, and its breadth was a stadium
everywhere; it was carried round the whole of the plain, and was
ten thousand stadia in length. It received the streams which
came down from the mountains, and winding round the plain and
touching the city at various points, was there let off into the sea.
From above, likewise, straight canals of a hundred feet in width
were cut in the plain, and again let off into the ditch towards the

sea: these canals were at intervals of an hundred stadia, and by
them they brought down the wood from the mountains to the
city; and conveyed the fruit of the earth in ships, cutting trans-
verse passages from one canal into another, and to the city.
Twice in the year they gathered the fruits of the earth—in
winter having the benefit of the rains, and in summer introducing
the water of the canals.

As to the population, each of the lots in the plain had an
appointed chief of men who were fit for military service, and the
size of the lot was to be a square of ten stadia each way, and
the total number of all the lots was sixty thousand. And of the
inhabitants of the mountains and of the rest of the country there
was also a vast multitude having leaders, to whom they were
assigned according to their dwellings and villages. The leader
was required to furnish for the war the sixth portion of a war-
chariot, so as to make up a total of ten thousand chariots; also
two horses and riders upon them, and a light chariot without a
seat, accompanied by a fighting man on foot carrying a small
shield, and having a charioteer mounted to guide the horses;
also, he was bound to furnish two heavy armed, two archers, two
slingers, three stone-shooters, and three javelin-men, who were
skirmishers, and four sailors to make up the complement of
twelve hundred ships. Such was the order of war in the royal
city—that of the other nine governments was different in each of
them, and would be wearisome to narrate.

As to offices and honours, the following was the arrangement
from the first. Each of the ten kings in his own division and in his
own city had the absolute control of the citizens, and in many
cases, of the laws, punishing and slaying whomsoever he would.
Now the relations of their governments to one another were
regulated by the injunctions of Poseidon as the law had handed
them down. These were inscribed by the first men on a column of
orichalcum, which was situated in the middle of the island, at the
temple of Poseidon, whither the people were gathered together
every fifth and sixth years alternately, thus giving equal honour
to the odd and to the even number. And when they were
gathered together they consulted about public affairs, and
enquired if any one had transgressed in anything, and passed
judgment on him accordingly, and before they passed judgment
they gave their pledges to one another on this wise: There were
bulls who had the range of the temple of Poseidon; and the ten
who were left alone in the temple, after they had offered prayers

to the gods that they might take the sacrifices which were acceptable to them, hunted the bulls, without weapons, but with staves and nooses; and the bull which they caught they led up to the column; the victim was then struck on the head by them and slain over the sacred inscription. Now on the column, besides the law, there was inscribed an oath invoking mighty curses on the disobedient. When, therefore, after offering sacrifice according to their customs, they had burnt the limbs of the bull, they mingled a cup and cast in a clot of blood for each of them; the rest of the victim they took to the fire, after having made a purification of the column all round. Then they drew from the cup in golden vessels, and pouring a libation on the fire, they swore that they would judge according to the laws on the column, and would punish anyone who had previously transgressed, and that for the future they would not, if they could help, transgress any of the inscriptions, and would not command or obey any ruler who commanded them, to act otherwise than according to the laws of their father Poseidon. This was the prayer which each of them offered up for himself and for his family, at the same time drinking and dedicating the vessel in the temple of the god, and after spending some necessary time at supper, when darkness came on, and the fire about the sacrifice was cool, all of them put on most beautiful azure robes, and, sitting on the ground, at night, near the embers of the sacrifices on which they had sworn, and extinguishing all the fire about the temple, they received and gave judgment, if any of them had any accusation to bring against anyone; and when they had given judgment, at daybreak, they wrote down their sentences on a golden tablet and deposited them as memorials with their robes.

There were many special laws which the several kings had inscribed about the temples, but the most important was the following: That they were not to take up arms against one another, and they were all to come to the rescue if any one in any city attempted to overthrow the royal house; like their ancestors, they were to deliberate in common about war and other matters, giving the supremacy to the family of Atlas. And the king was not to have the power of life and death over any of his kinsmen unless he had the assent of the majority of the ten kings.

Such was the vast power which the god settled in the lost island of Atlantis; and this he afterwards directed against our land on the following pretext, as traditions tell. For many generations, as long as the divine nature lasted in them, they were obedient to the laws, and well-affectioned towards the gods, who were their kinsmen; for they possessed true and in every way great spirits, practising gentleness and wisdom in the various chances of life, and in their intercourse with one another. They despised everything but virtue, not caring for their present state of life, and thinking lightly of the possession of gold and other property, which seemed only a burden to them; neither were they intoxicated by luxury; nor did wealth deprive them of their self-control; but they were sober, and saw clearly that all these goods are increased by virtuous friendship with one another, and that by excessive zeal for them, and honour of them, the good of them is lost and friendship perishes with them. By such reflections and by the continuance in them of a divine nature, all that which we have described waxed and increased in them; but when this divine portion began to fade away in them, and became diluted too often and with too much of the mortal admixture, and the human nature got the upper hand, then they, being unable to bear their fortune, became unseemly, and to him who had an eye to see, they began to appear base, and had lost the fairest of their precious gifts; but to those who had no eye to see the true happiness, they still appeared glorious and blessed at the very time when they were filled with unrighteous avarice and power. Zeus, the god of gods, who rules with law, and is able to see into such things, perceiving that an honourable race was in a most wretched state, and wanting to inflict punishment on them, that they might be chastened and improve, collected all the gods into his most holy habitation, which being placed in the centre of the world, sees all things that partake of generation. And when he had called them together, he spoke as follows:

With these words Plato ended his report. According to Plutarch it was Plato's death which prevented the great Greek from finishing his work.

*These extracts are taken from* The Dialogues of Plato, *translated by B. Jowett, and published at the Clarendon Press, Oxford.*